Four Decades of Poverty Reduction in China

Four Decades of Poverty Reduction in China

Drivers, Insights for the World, and the Way Ahead

The World Bank

Development Research Center of the State Council, the People's Republic of China

Contents

Foreword . . . . *ix*

Acknowledgments . . . . *xi*

Executive Summary . . . . *xiii*

Abbreviations . . . . *xvii*

1 Introduction 1
Context 1
Notes 3
References 4

2 Forty Years of Rural Poverty Reduction 5
Introduction 5
What drove poverty reduction in China? 6
Notes 9
References 9

3 Drivers of China's Economic Transformation and Poverty Reduction . . . 11
Introduction 11
Growing agricultural productivity: Higher incomes and more choices 13
Progressive industrialization: Better jobs for more people 16
Managed urbanization: Multiple gains for migrants and nonmigrant rural families,
but persistent inequality of opportunities 21
Expanded infrastructure investment: Improved connectivity and job creation for
the poor 25
Notes 27
References 31

4   Poverty Alleviation Strategies...................................37

Introduction...37
Area-based poverty alleviation strategies......................38
Social protection policies....................................40
Targeted poverty alleviation strategy.........................42
Notes...49
References..50

5   Implications of China's Poverty Reduction 53

China's approach to poverty reduction in a global context..........53
References..56

6   The Way Ahead..59

Introduction...59
New drivers of growth and poverty reduction.....................59
Defining new standards and policy objectives for a prosperous China 61
Coordinating pro-poor development policies and social protection programs 62
Notes...63
References..63

7   Conclusions..65

Concluding remarks 65
References..67

Appendix A: Key Household Surveys...............................69

Boxes

3.1   Agricultural technology extension for poverty reduction: Promoting
       mulch film in Guyuan 16
3.2   Upgrading skills through learning by doing: How Mr. Xie Dewu set up his
       own valve-making company in Yongjia..................................19
4.1   The evolution of poverty targeting: How China used international expertise......39
4.2   Human resources and incentives for targeted poverty alleviation 44
4.3   East-West collaboration from the perspective of a poverty-stricken district
       in Ningxia Autonomous Region 45
4.4   How digital technologies were leveraged for targeted poverty alleviation........47
5.1   China's poverty reduction policies as a case study in pro-poor governance.......55

Figures

ES.1   The two pillars of China's approach to poverty reduction.................. xiv
1.1   Poverty reduction in China over the past 40 years based on the 2010 poverty
       standard..2
1.2   China accounts for almost three-quarters of global extreme poverty reduction
       since 1981: Poverty headcount based on the international poverty line, 1981–2017 3
2.1   Rapid economic growth drove poverty reduction 7
2.2   Drivers of rural poverty reduction, 1988–2018 7

3.1 Rapid and sustained economic growth in China came about with fast economic transformation, 1978–2018 12

3.2 Labor productivity, particularly from industry, drove high economic growth, 1995–2018 17

3.3 Employment and productivity of manufacturing, 1978–2001 18

3.4 Workers benefited from the diversification of jobs and the expansion of wage employment, 1998–2013 20

3.5 Wage gaps between urban and rural areas narrowed, suggesting that China reached the Lewis tipping point around 2007 21

3.6 Urbanization in China followed a similar pattern as other fast-growing economies, 1960–2019 22

3.7 Migration has increased consistently over time, as have migrant earnings as a share of total household income, 1993–2017 23

3.8 "Floating" populations' income per month 24

3.9 Infrastructure investment grew steadily beginning in the early 1990s. 26

4.1 Central and provincial Anti-Poverty Fund allocations, 2001–20. 44

Tables

2.1 Poverty reduction between 1978 and 2019 6

4.1 Main social protection programs in rural and urban China, 2019 or latest available data 41

4.2 Share of registered poor households achieving "three guarantees" and safe drinking water 49

Foreword

Over the past 40 years, the number of people in China with incomes below US$1.90 per day has fallen by close to 800 million, accounting for close to three-quarters of global poverty reduction since 1980. At China's current poverty standards, the number of poor people in China fell by 770 million. By any measure, the speed and scale of China's poverty reduction is historically unprecedented.

In 2019, the Ministry of Finance, the Development Research Center of the State Council, and the World Bank decided to take stock of this achievement. A group of staff from the China Center for International Knowledge on Development (CIKD) and the World Bank was tasked with this assessment. Their work, supported by academic research and numerous background papers, is summarized in this report. The report looks at the key drivers of China's poverty alleviation, considers the insights of China's poverty reduction experience for other developing countries, and puts forward suggestions for China's future policy direction.

The main conclusion is that China's poverty reduction success relied mainly on two pillars. The first pillar was rapid economic growth, supported by broad-based economic transformation, which provided new economic opportunities for the poor and raised average incomes. The second pillar was government policies to alleviate persistent poverty, which initially targeted areas disadvantaged by geography and a lack of economic opportunities, but subsequently focused on poor households, irrespective of their location. China's success benefited from effective governance, which was key to the successful implementation of the growth strategy as well as the evolving set of targeted poverty reduction policies. China also benefited from some favorable initial conditions at the time of opening up, such as a relatively high level of human capital.

This report points to a number of lessons from China's experience for other countries, including the importance of focusing on education, export orientation, sustained public investment in infrastructure, and structural policies that support market competition. With an eye on the future, this report considers the likely structural shifts in China's future growth model, including rebalancing toward consumption and high-value services and embarking on a carbon-neutral development path, and it discusses the implications of these transitions for China's future policy agenda. Finally, it highlights the need to close remaining gaps in quality education between rural and urban areas, to provide better social protection to migrant workers, and to widen the scope for improved integration of the various existing social security policies to address errors of exclusion and improve overall efficiency.

The work summarized in this report took place over more than two years. The team held a series of workshops and several discussions with government agencies as well as relevant domestic and international experts and scholars. The research team conducted field visits in Ningxia and Zhejiang and received inputs from other local governments, which informed in-depth qualitative research on the changes and effectiveness of poverty reduction policies over the past 40 years. The report also benefited from the support of the National Bureau of Statistics of China and the China Household Income Project, which provided access to household survey data. The overall project resulted in more than 20 background studies, including quantitative analysis, case studies, and qualitative evaluations of the effectiveness of policy implementation. This report summarizes the main findings of these multiple studies.

This report stands in a good tradition of joint research between the World Bank and the Development Research Center of the State Council. Starting with the *China 2030* study, published in 2012, these joint reports have aimed at synthesizing the views of researchers on both sides and achieving a basic consensus on key policy issues. The benefit of carrying out a joint research effort lies as much in the—sometimes lively—discussions preceding the drafting of the final report with the aim to better understand each other as in the final draft itself. We hope that the present report, *Four Decades of Poverty Reduction in China: Drivers, Insights for the World, and the Way Ahead* will enhance the understanding of China's development path over the past four decades and become a useful reference for poverty reduction practitioners around the world.

LU Hao
President and Party Secretary,
Development Research Center of the
State Council,
People's Republic of China

Manuela Ferro
Vice President for East Asia and the
Pacific Region,
World Bank

Acknowledgments

This report was undertaken at the joint initiative of China's Ministry of Finance (MOF) and the World Bank. It was jointly led by the World Bank and the Development Research Center of the State Council (DRC). Minister Kun Liu from the MOF, President Hao Lu from the DRC, and former Party Secretary Jiantang Ma from the DRC provided overall guidance. As the Chinese implementing agency, the Center for International Knowledge on Development (CIKD) affiliated with the DRC conducted the research closely with the World Bank. The team benefited from detailed guidance from former Vice Minister Jiayi Zou, Vice Minister Weiping Yu from the MOF, and Vice President Laiming Zhang from the DRC. On the World Bank side, it was guided by the Country Director for China and Mongolia, Martin Raiser; the Director for Equitable Growth, Finance and Institutions for the East Asia and Pacific Region, Hassan Zaman; and the Program Manager for Poverty and Equity in the East Asia and Pacific Region, Rinku Murgai. On the DRC side, the work was guided by CIKD President Changwen Zhao and former Executive Vice-President Gong Sen.

This synthesis report brings together the findings of four technical papers prepared by a World Bank team, a separate report prepared by the CIKD, and several background studies commissioned by the CIKD. The synthesis was prepared by Maria Ana Lugo, Martin Raiser, and Ruslan Yemtsov from the World Bank, and Gong Sen, Xiaomin Liang, and Changwen Zhao from the CIKD. The analytical findings were discussed at a series of joint workshops with participation from international experts. The joint teams consulted relevant government agencies, including the Ministry of Foreign Affairs, the MOF, the National Development and Reform Commission, the Ministry of Industry and Information Technology, the Ministry of Human Resources and Social Security, the Ministry of Agriculture and Rural Affairs, the Ministry of Commerce, the National Bureau of Statistics, and the National Administration for Rural Revitalization (formerly known as the State Council Leading Group of Poverty Alleviation and Development). The report benefited from thorough reviews, comments, and editorial suggestions from project leaders and reviewers, including, among others, Sebastian Eckardt, Samuel Freije-Rodriguez, Ruth Hill, Andrew Mason, Aaditya Mattoo, Ambar Narayan, Philip O'Keefe, and Xiaolin Wang. The team also organized several rounds of reviews, including the technical workshop that brought together the authors of the background studies and experts working on various aspects of China's poverty reduction. In addition, the report benefited from valuable inputs from Yang Huang, Yoonhee Kim, Ladisy Komba Chengula, Ren Mu, Mark Roberts, Dewen Wang, Xiaolan Wang, Jin Zhang, Luan Zhao, and Min Zhao (CIKD).

The Chinese translation was done by Mixiang Pang and reviewed by Yang Huang and Chiyu Niu. Excellent support at various stages of work was provided by Tianshu Chen and Tianxiu Kang from the World Bank office in Beijing. Patricia Katayama and Mark McClure managed the publication of the English version of the final report. The Global Corporate Solutions unit managed the production and design of the conference edition of the report.

The World Bank team of authors of technical papers and background studies includes Samuel Freije-Rodriguez, John Giles, Hanchen Jiang, Maria Ana Lugo, Dino Merotto, Ren Mu, Chiyu Niu, Ruslan Yemtsov, and Fuchang Zhao. The CIKD team of authors includes Xiao Chen, Sen Gong, Dengsheng Hu, Ruoyun Hua, Xiheng Jiang, Bingqin Li, Cangshu Li, Shi Li, Xiaomin Liang, Changyu Liu, Chen Liu, Haibo Long, Tianyue Ma, Chuanliang Shen, Qiu Shen, Yangyang Shen, Xiaolin Wang, Puheyan Xu, Lvjun Zhou, Taidong Zhou, Yu Zhou, and Qingyi Zhu.

The team would like to acknowledge the support provided by the National Bureau of Statistics, China Household Income Project team, comprising Dr. Shi Li and Dr. Peng Zhan from Zhejiang University. The research team would like to thank Yuanzhou District of Ningxia Hui Autonomous Region and Yongjia County of Zhejiang province for their valuable assistance in the field research, as well as Minhe County of Qinghai province, Daming County of Hebei province, and Xunwu County of Jiangxi province, for their contributions of data. The team benefited from overarching guidance and advice from World Bank management, the Ministry of Finance Directorate, and DRC leadership.

Executive Summary

Overview

Over the past 40 years, the number of people in China with incomes below US$1.90 per day—the international poverty line as defined by the World Bank to track global extreme poverty—has fallen by close to 800 million. With this, China has accounted for almost 75 percent of the global reduction in the number of people living in extreme poverty. In 2021, China declared that it has eradicated extreme poverty according to the national poverty threshold, lifting 770 million people out of poverty since 1978, and that it has built a "moderately prosperous society in all respects." Whether measured with the international or national poverty line, the speed and scale of China's poverty reduction is historically unprecedented. Although China has eradicated extreme poverty, a significant number of people remain vulnerable, with incomes below a threshold more typically used to define poverty in upper-middle-income countries. China has set a new goal of achieving significant progress toward *common prosperity* by 2035.[1] While no particular income target or poverty threshold is attached to this goal, it can help keep the policy focus on the vulnerable population over the coming decade.

This synthesis report aims to explore the key drivers for China's poverty alleviation achievements in the past 40 years and to consider the lessons of China's experience for other developing countries. In addition, it put foward suggestions for China's future policies. China's approach to poverty reduction was based on two pillars (see figure ES.1). The first pillar aimed for broad-based economic transformation to open new economic opportunities and raise average incomes. The second pillar was the recognition that targeted support was needed to alleviate persistent poverty; support was initially provided to areas disadvantaged by geography and the lack of opportunities and then later to individual households. The success of China's economic development and the associated reduction of poverty benefited from effective governance, which helped coordinate multiple government agencies and induce cooperation from nongovernment stakeholders. To illustrate the role of broad-based economic transformation for poverty alleviation, separate sections of this report respectively analyze growing agricultural productivity, incremental industrialization, managed urbanization and rural-to-urban migration, and the role of infrastructure. The evolution of China's approach to poverty alleviation,

FIGURE ES.1   **The two pillars of China's approach to poverty reduction**

Source: World Bank and Center for International Knowledge on Development.

from place-based to countrywide social protection policies, and the targeted poverty alleviation strategy under implementation since 2012 are also reviewed.

China's poverty reduction story is primarily a growth story. China's rapid and sustained economic growth has been accompanied by a broad-based economic transformation. Reforms began in the agricultural sector, where poor people could benefit directly from improvements in productivity associated with the introduction of market incentives. The development of low-skilled, labor-intensive industries provided a source of employment for workers released from agriculture. Urbanization helped migrants take advantage of the new opportunities in the cities, and migrant transfers boosted incomes of their relatives remaining in the villages. Public investment in infrastructure improved living conditions in rural areas but also connected them with urban and export markets. Reforms in all these areas were incremental, which may have helped businesses and the population adjust to the rapid pace of change. Government policies targeted specifically to poverty reduction have also played an important role in improving the lives of poor people in rural areas, particularly after the poverty headcount dropped below 10 percent of the rural population, and contributed to the eradication of extreme poverty by 2020.

China's success in poverty reduction was supported by effective governance. Like its East Asian peers, China has been endowed with a capable and effective government, able to credibly commit to the target of poverty reduction, facilitate interagency coordination within and across various levels of government in implementing policies, and mobilize nongovernment stakeholders to cooperate in achieving policy objectives. The institutional arrangements China developed to deliver outcomes were shaped by its specific context. Thus, China's size necessitated decentralized implementation arrangements, with significant scope for local experimentation, and a high degree of competition among local governments. To achieve coherence, however, local experimentation was subject to strong monitoring and accountability between levels of government, with high-powered administrative incentives for public officials.

Rapid economic growth since the launch of reform and opening up in 1978 can be partially attributed to favorable initial conditions, including a relatively well-educated and healthy population, low fertility rates, a high saving rate, and equitable land distribution. China shared some of these characteristics with other fast-growing economies, particularly those in East Asia, and to some extent the pace of poverty reduction since 1980 reflects China catching up with regional peers. Key elements of China's reform and opening up policies also mirrored those adopted in high-growth economies elsewhere. These include an emphasis on human capital accumulation, outward orientation, public investments in infrastructure, macroeconomic stability, and structural policies generally consistent with comparative advantages and supportive of competition.

The eradication of extreme poverty is not the end of China's poverty reduction agenda. Instead, the focus will now need to shift toward closing remaining gaps in access to quality services, addressing persistent inequality of incomes and economic opportunities, and mitigating the risks for the most vulnerable associated with the expected continued economic transformation toward a greener, more urban, and more service-oriented economy. Adjusting the national poverty threshold once again to reflect China's rising income level could be part of a new policy framework leading the country toward the goal of *common prosperity* by 2035. The further integration of targeted poverty reduction measures with China's social protection system would help ensure that all who are vulnerable receive adequate support and would limit the risk that some may unduly benefit more than others. Many of these priorities are reflected in the 2021 Government Work Report[2] with specific actions to be developed during the implementation of the 14th Five-Year Plan.

Finally, this review of China's poverty reduction experience leaves a number of questions open for further research. First, the interplay between poverty reduction and growth deserves further analysis to understand the extent that poverty reduction measures may, in turn, help less-developed areas grow faster and help poor people participate in economic activities. This understanding could be of relevance, for example, for other middle-income countries with pockets of poverty. Second, a deeper analysis of China's use of policy experimentation at the local level combined with high-powered performance incentives may contribute to our understanding of models of decentralization and public service delivery. Third, an evaluation of China's targeted poverty alleviation experience in recent years would benefit from further analysis of individual policy interventions and their interactions to better understand not just the effectiveness but also the efficiency and sustainability of the program. An analysis of the costs and benefits of policy intervention would also be warranted in a broader sense, helping to systematically account (*suan da zhang* in the Chinese term) for factors such as the impact of infrastructure investments on poverty reduction or the merits of the *hukou* system and managed urbanization policies. In all these areas, active exchanges between researchers within and outside of China, and between academics and policy makers, should be encouraged, and the data needed for high-quality empirical work should be made more widely available. These actions will help ensure that China's poverty reduction achievements get the attention and understanding that they deserve.

Notes

1. The term "common prosperity" (*gong tong fu yu* in Chinese) was first coined by Mao Zedong in the early 1950s, aimed at achieving shared prosperity in rural areas. In the late 1970s, Deng Xiaoping reiterated the concept, taking a phased approach to the implementation of reforms ("We can allow some people to become rich first; those who become rich first can help the others and eventually achieve common prosperity"). In 2021, President Xi Jinping set out a timeline for realizing equal access to basic public services by 2035 and for common prosperity to be "basically achieved" by 2050.
2. "Report on the Work of the Government" (https://english.www.gov.cn/atts/stream/files/622c9400c6 d0cc300eea7894).

Abbreviations

APF	Anti-Poverty Fund
ASPIRE	Atlas of Social Protection Indicators of Resilience and Equity
CHIP	Chinese Household Income Project
CIKD	Center for International Knowledge on Development
DRC	Development Research Center of the State Council (China)
EAP	East Asia and Pacific
GDP	gross domestic product
GNI	gross national income
ILO	International Labour Organization
MOF	Ministry of Finance
NBS	National Bureau of Statistics (China)
OECD	Organisation for Economic Co-operation and Development
PPP	purchasing power parity
RMB	renminbi
TVEs	township and village enterprises
UN	United Nations
UNDP	United Nations Development Programme
WDI	World Development Indicators
WTO	World Trade Organization

1

Introduction

Context

China's economic growth and poverty reduction over the past 40 years are historically unprecedented, both in speed and scale. Between 1978 and 2019, the proportion of people living in poverty—as per the national 2010 standard—fell from 97.5 percent to 0.6 percent of the rural population (figure 1.1, panel a).[1] The poverty headcount dropped from 770 million to 5.5 million people,[2] that is, 765 million fewer poor people after four decades. In other words, on average, per year there were 19 million fewer poor people over 40 years (with an average decline of 2.4 percentage points per year). Measured by the US$1.90 poverty line (2011 purchasing power parity), the headcount rate dropped from 88.1 percent in 1981 to 0.3 percent by the end of 2018. The total population lifted out of poverty was nearly 800 million over this period. If one considers higher poverty lines, such as those typically used in lower-middle- and upper-middle-income countries, poverty in China declined rapidly and continuously as well—albeit more slowly than when using the national standard (figure 1.1, panel b). On February 25, 2021, the government announced that it had reached its goal of eliminating rural extreme poverty.[3]

Decades of progress in China are also reflected in substantial improvements in other measures of well-being. At the start of reforms in 1978, life expectancy at birth at 66 years already far exceeded that of other developing countries (UNDP, China Institute for Development Planning at Tsinghua University, and State Information Center 2019), placing the country in a favorable starting position. Health outcomes continued to improve over the four subsequent decades, with life expectancy reaching 77 years by 2019, and the infant mortality rate dropping from 52 in 1978 to 6.8 per thousand infants in 2019 (World Development Indicators). Education achievements in China were also relatively higher than in its peers prior to 1978 and progressed further since, as the country universalized basic and secondary education. By 2010, China had reached 88 percent enrollment in secondary education, closing the gap with upper-middle-income countries such as Brazil and South Africa, despite having still considerably lower gross domestic product (GDP) per capita. The share of adults that completed lower secondary education almost tripled from 22.8 percent in 1982 to 65.3 percent in 2010 (World Development Indicators).

FIGURE 1.1   **Poverty reduction in China over the past 40 years based on the 2010 poverty standard**

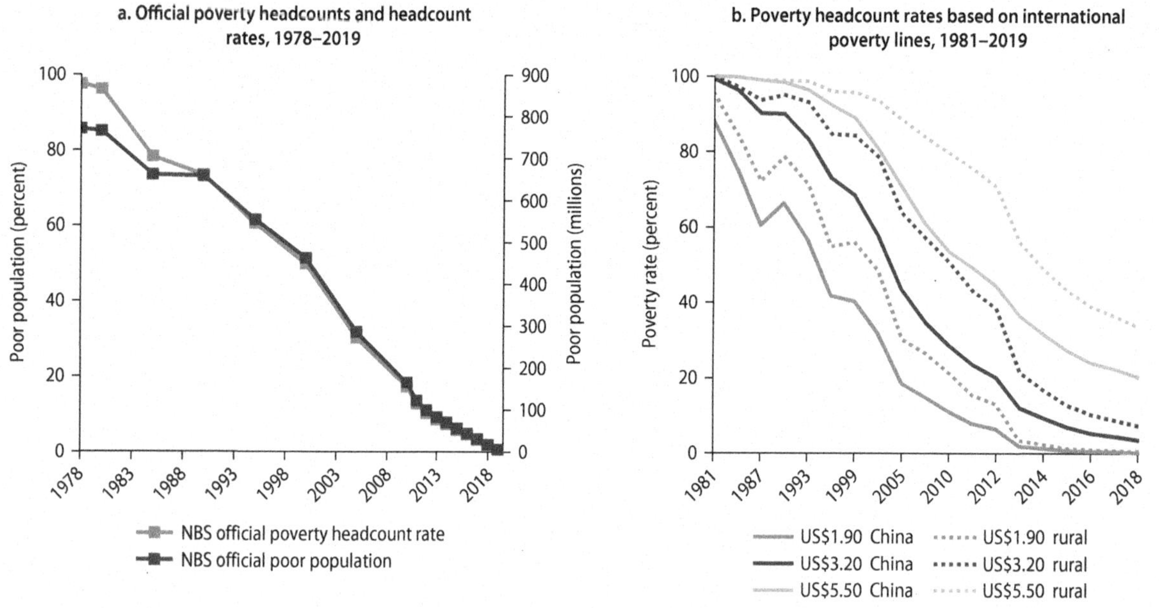

a. Official poverty headcounts and headcount rates, 1978–2019

b. Poverty headcount rates based on international poverty lines, 1981–2019

— NBS official poverty headcount rate
— NBS official poor population

US$1.90 China ······ US$1.90 rural
US$3.20 China ······ US$3.20 rural
US$5.50 China ······ US$5.50 rural

Sources: Lugo, Niu, and Yemtsov 2021. Panel a is based on the official poverty headcount rate for rural areas from China Statistical Yearbooks (NBS) using the 2010 standard—equivalent to US$2.30 per person per day, 2011 purchasing power parity. Panel b is based on PovcalNet 1981–2019, based on NBS grouped data. The US$1.90 per day threshold is the international poverty line; the US$3.20 per day line is typical of lower-middle-income countries; and the US$5.50 per day line is typical of upper-middle-income countries.
Note: NBS = National Bureau of Statistics.

Taken together, improvements in health, education, and income over the four decades are reflected in China's rising position in the Human Development Index from 106 (out of 144 countries) in 1990 to 85 (out of 189 countries) in 2019, and the narrowing of the gaps with other large developing countries (UNDP, China Institute for Development Planning at Tsinghua University, and State Information Center 2019). Multidimensional (nonmonetary) poverty has also improved over the past decades. According to the United Nations Development Programme's multidimensional poverty measure, the share of poor people fell from 12.5 percent in 2002 to 3.9 in 2014 (UNDP, China Institute for Development Planning at Tsinghua University, and State Information Center 2019).

China's eradication of extreme poverty is of global importance. Its achievement in poverty reduction helped the world attain the Millennium Development Goals set for 2015. In the first five years since then, China has achieved the first United Nations (UN) Sustainable Development Goal, target 1.1, of eradicating extreme poverty 10 years ahead of schedule. Between 1981 and 2017, using the international poverty line (US$1.90 per person per day, 2011 purchasing power parity), on average, there were almost 34 million fewer poor people in the world each year, with 24 million of them coming from China. China alone accounts for almost three-quarters of the total reduction in global extreme poverty in that period (figure 1.2). The pace of poverty reduction in China has been consistently faster than in the rest of the world, considered as a whole.

The present report reviews China's poverty reduction practices and experience over the past four decades and depicts the major driving forces behind it. It does so by combining new quantitative and qualitative analyses and a review of the existing literature.[4] The qualitative analyses include in-depth interviews with households as well as with representatives of villages, enterprises, and county officials from two sample counties—Guyuan County (now Yuanzhou District) of Ningxia Hui Autonomous Region and Yongjia County of Zhejiang province—that help provide a better understanding of the effects of policies, considering the voices of those engaged in both policy making and policy implementation. In addition, this study also discusses China's post-2020 antipoverty policies. Unlike in most other countries in the world, poverty in China is officially defined only for rural areas, given that the share of the urban poor has traditionally been very small.[5] Following the official definition, the report focuses primarily on factors that improved the living standards of rural households. It is intended to inform audiences in other countries about China's efforts and motivate future policy reforms in China itself (including China's rapidly increasing development aid to low-income countries).

The report is structured as follows. Chapter 2 describes the relationship between economic growth and poverty reduction over the four decades since 1978 and shows the contribution to poverty reduction of each household income component to set the scene for the rest of the report. Chapter 3 addresses the drivers of broad-based economic transformation, namely, growing agricultural productivity, incremental industrialization, managed urbanization and rural-to-urban migration, and the supportive role of infrastructure in that process. Chapter 4 summarizes the role of poverty alleviation strategies and programs over the years, including development-oriented area-based poverty programs, social protection policies, and the recent targeted poverty alleviation strategy. Chapter 5 considers the implications of China's experience of poverty reduction for a global audience, and chapter 6 provides a reflection on themes that are likely to shape the debate over poverty reduction in China going forward. Chapter 7 provides conclusions.

FIGURE 1.2 China accounts for almost three-quarters of global extreme poverty reduction since 1981: Poverty headcount based on the international poverty line, 1981–2017

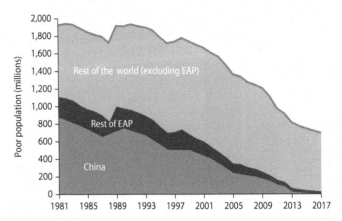

Sources: Lugo, Niu, and Yemtsov 2021, based on PovcalNet adapted from World Bank 2018.
Note: EAP = East Asia and Pacific.

Notes

1. Poverty in China is defined only among the rural population, reflecting a long-standing view that in China poverty is "fundamentally a rural phenomenon," as the share of the urban poor tends to be very small (Naughton 2018). For comparability over time, poverty is measured using a poverty line known as the "2010 Standard" (2,300 RMB/year in 2010), reported by the National Bureau of Statistics (NBS) Statistical Yearbook. Yet, it should be noted that two other standards have been used in the past, the 1978 Standard (206 RMB/year in 1985) and the 2008 Standard (865 RMB/year in 2000) that were more relevant at the time, given the country's level of income. Using these lower lines, poverty has followed a similar pattern of continued decline, although they indicate a more noticeable slowdown in poverty reduction toward the end of the 1990s and into the mid-2000s.

2. Number of the people living in poverty as reported in the 2020 NBS Statistical Yearbook. The calculation of the number of the people living in poverty also considers the population residing in urban areas but with rural *hukou*, consistent with the sampling frame used by the Rural Household Survey until 2012.

3. "China Celebrates Official End of Extreme Poverty, Lauds Xi," AP News, https://apnews.com/article /china-celebrates-end-extreme-poverty-1449b5dc8a48483af847f4c38f64c326.

4. The literature on China's poverty reduction is large both in Chinese and in English. This overview does not aim to be a complete survey of this literature. It nonetheless aims to show where a broad consensus has been established on the drivers of China's poverty reduction and where the debate remains open and additional work is needed.

5. For instance, Chen and Ravallion (2021) estimate that, once cost-of-living differences are accounted for, income poverty in 1985, based on the poverty standard at the time, was less than 1 percent in urban areas, compared with 24 percent in rural areas.

References

Chen, Shaohua, and Martin Ravallion. 2021. "Reconciling the Conflicting Narratives on Poverty in China." *Journal of Development Economics* 153 (November): 102711.

Lugo, Maria Ana, Chiyu Niu, and Ruslan Yemtsov. 2021. "China's Poverty Reduction and Economic Transformation: A Decomposition Approach." Policy Research Working Paper 9849, World Bank, Washington, DC.

Naughton, Barry. 2018. *The Chinese Economy: Adaptation and Growth.* Second edition. Cambridge, MA: MIT Press.

UNDP (United Nations Development Programme), China Institute for Development Planning at Tsinghua University, and State Information Center. 2019. *China National Human Development Report Special Edition—In Pursuit of a More Sustainable Future for All: China's Historic Transformation over Four Decades of Human Development.* Beijing: China Publishing Group Corporation, China Translation & Publishing House.

World Bank. 2018a. *Poverty and Shared Prosperity 2018: Piecing Together the Poverty Puzzle.* Washington, DC: World Bank.

2

Forty Years of Rural Poverty Reduction

Introduction

China's poverty reduction story since the late 1970s is fundamentally a growth story, complemented, particularly in more recent years, by targeted poverty reduction policies and programs.[1] From 1978 to 2020, China's per capita gross domestic product (GDP) grew 8.2 percent per year on average while the poverty rate fell by 2.3 percentage points per year.[2] Economywide policies implemented since 1978 spurred rapid economic growth, improving agricultural productivity and expanding nonagricultural sectors, which created more and better-paying jobs. Accompanied by an accelerated demographic transition, increased migration from rural to urban areas, and the significant expansion in access to physical infrastructure as well as education and health care, the process of structural change allowed the poor to take advantage of emerging economic opportunities. In the past decade, when the share of poor people in rural areas fell below 10 percent, targeted poverty alleviation policies became more important.

Rural poverty declined consistently over the four decades since 1978. Based on the official 2010 poverty standard applied to the rural population only, on average, there were 18.7 million fewer poor people in China every year since 1978 (table 2.1). The largest yearly decline was in the 2000s, when economic growth reached almost 10 percent and close to 30 million people were lifted out of poverty every year. Poverty reduction continued to be strong after 2010, even as economic growth slowed, thus reflecting a higher growth elasticity of poverty. Since 2013, as the rural poverty rate fell below 10 percent, the annual average fall in the number of poor people naturally declined at a time when per capita GDP growth also slowed.

For every percentage point of economic growth, rural poverty has declined, on average, by 1.4 percent. High and sustained growth has brought significant income gains across the distribution, making growth shared. However, China does not stand out in terms of the efficiency with which growth was translated into poverty reduction (what is known as the elasticity of poverty with respect to growth or the growth elasticity of poverty). Indeed, fast growth came alongside increasing inequality, driven by rising urban-rural disparities as well as disparities across regions, which reduced the effect of growth on poverty reduction, at least until 2010.

TABLE 2.1   **Poverty reduction between 1978 and 2019**

	Rural poverty						Per capita GDP growth (percent, annualized)	Growth semi-elasticity of poverty	Growth elasticity of poverty
				Change					
				Absolute change		Relative change (percent, annualized)			
Year	Headcount (million)	Rate (percentage)	Period	(million per year)	(percentage points per year)				
1978	770	97.5							
1990	658	73.5	1978–1990	−9.3	−2.0	−2.3	7.5	−0.27	−0.31
2000	462	49.8	1990–2000	−19.6	−2.4	−3.8	9.3	−0.26	−0.41
2010	166	17.2	2000–2010	−29.7	−3.3	−10.1	9.9	−0.33	−1.02
2013	82	8.5	2010–2013	−27.7	−2.9	−20.9	7.9	−0.37	−2.66
2019	6	0.6	2013–2019	−12.8	−1.3	−35.7	6.3	−0.21	−5.64
			1978–2019	−18.7	−2.4	−11.7	8.4	−0.28	−1.40

Source: Lugo, Niu, and Yemtsov 2021, based on National Bureau of Statistics Yearbook using 2010 standard for poverty rates, and World Development Indicators for GDP per capita growth (constant 2010 US$).
Note: Growth elasticity of poverty is the percentage change in poverty headcount rates associated with a 1 percentage point change in per capita GDP. Semi-elasticity is defined as the percentage point change in the poverty headcount rate for a 1 percent change in per capita GDP. GDP = gross domestic product.

The income-based Gini index rose from 30 in the mid-1980s to 49.1 in 2008, and then began to decrease.[3] Interpersonal disparities increased as the country moved to a market economy. Had the distribution not changed between 1990 and 2010, poverty would have declined an additional 6 percentage points (figure 2.1, panel a). Once inequality is controlled for, the growth elasticity of poverty is –2.7 in the case of per capita GDP, much higher than the –1.45 unconditional estimate (Lugo, Niu, and Yemtsov 2021).[4]

More than the ability to translate growth into poverty reduction, it was China's sustained fast growth that was unusual by international standards and that makes its poverty reduction record stand out. Compared with other countries with data available for at least 20 years, China's semi-elasticity[5] of poverty with respect to economic growth, a statistic better suited to making international comparisons when initial poverty rates differ widely, is fairly high, although other countries, such as Brazil, Indonesia, Pakistan, and South Africa, show significantly higher levels. What makes China unique is its ability to continuously grow fast over several decades, as seen in figure 2.1 (panel b).[6]

What drove poverty reduction in China?

Based on a poverty decomposition exercise that describes the changes in poverty in terms of the associated changes in household incomes by income sources, the following features emerge:

Starting from very high poverty headcount rates (over four-fifths of the total rural population), the growth in agricultural incomes was initially the main driving force behind poverty reduction. From a household perspective, rising labor income was the largest contributor to poverty reduction between 1988 and 2007 (figure 2.2). In the initial years, rising agricultural productivity alone was the most important factor behind the change in poverty.[7] Real earnings per unit of labor in the agricultural sector grew at an annual rate of 8 percent between 1988 and 1995, and a vast majority of the rural workforce (more than four out of five) remained engaged in agriculture.

Since the mid-1990s, the expansion of the nonagricultural sectors (in rural areas and through migration to urban areas) and rapidly rising productivity and earnings per worker started playing a more noticeable role in poverty reduction (figure 2.2). As discussed later in this report, evidence shows that the rise of Township and Village Enterprises (Naughton 2018; Riskin 1987), government investment (Fan, Zhang, and Zhang 2004; Fan and Chan-Kang 2005), the restructuring of the industrial sector, and the movement of rural workers to urban

FIGURE 2.1   **Rapid economic growth drove poverty reduction**

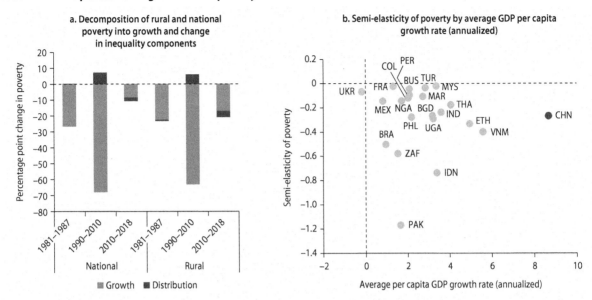

a. Decomposition of rural and national poverty into growth and change in inequality components

b. Semi-elasticity of poverty by average GDP per capita growth rate (annualized)

■ Growth   ■ Distribution

Sources: Panel a: Lugo, Niu, and Yemtsov 2021, based on PovcalNet, using the international poverty line (US$1.90 per day per person, 2011 purchasing power parity). Panel b: Lugo, Niu, and Yemtsov 2021, based on PovcalNet and World Development Indicators, using the international poverty line (US$1.90 per day per person, 2011 purchasing power parity) and per capita GDP (constant 2010 US$).
Note: Panel a: poverty decomposition following Datt and Ravallion (1992). Data available for 1981–87 are based on per capita disposable income, while 1990–2018 data are based on per capita household expenditure. The period 1990–2010 is a time of increasing inequality, while over 2010–18 inequality is declining. Panel b: Country abbreviations are International Standards Organization codes. Countries included are those with data on poverty headcount and per capita GDP available in a time span of more than 20 years, they have at least five data points within the time span, and have a population greater than 30 million. Semi-elasticity of growth with respect to per capita GDP is calculated using a regression-based approach. GDP = gross domestic product.

FIGURE 2.2   **Drivers of rural poverty reduction, 1988–2018**

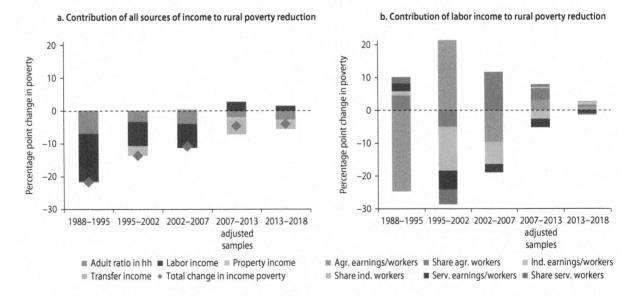

a. Contribution of all sources of income to rural poverty reduction

b. Contribution of labor income to rural poverty reduction

■ Adult ratio in hh   ■ Labor income   ■ Property income
■ Transfer income   ◆ Total change in income poverty

■ Agr. earnings/workers   ■ Share agr. workers   ■ Ind. earnings/workers
■ Share ind. workers   ■ Serv. earnings/workers   ■ Share serv. workers

Source: Lugo, Niu, and Yemtsov 2021, based on Chinese Household Income Project surveys (for more information on the survey, see appendix A).
Note: Shapley decomposition of poverty changes by income sources following Azevedo et al. (2013). Panel b further decomposes the labor income component by earnings per worker and share of workers in each economic sector. The 2007–2013 adjusted sample refers to the adjustment made to consider a break in comparability over time, as the sampling frame changed from being *hukou*-based (place of registration) to census-based (place of residence). After the adjustment, the "2007–2013 adjusted sample" is comparable to "2013–2018." agr. = agriculture; hh = household; ind. = industry; serv. = services.

jobs in coastal areas were some of the key factors that contributed to family income growth and helped lift millions out of poverty.

Over the years, the regional contributions to poverty reduction shifted from coastal areas to the western and central regions. The establishment of special economic zones and the Coastal Development Strategy in the mid-1980s followed the government's strategy to develop the country's more prosperous coastal provinces by boosting their participation in international trade and foreign direct investment flows. By 1999, the eastern region's GDP per capita was twice as high as in the rest of the country. Despite having a quarter of the country's poor in 1995, the region accounted for 40 percent of the total rural poverty reduction between 1995 and 2002, with 79 million fewer poor people.[8] In the 2000s, the government implemented the Western Development Program to close regional gaps by directing considerable government resources, including infrastructure investment, fiscal transfers, and subsidies, to lagging regions (Fan, Kanbur, and Zhang 2011). Consequently, the western region accounted for 50 percent of the total decline in rural poverty between 2002 and 2007 (while representing less than one-quarter of the country's population).

Since 2013, rural poverty had fallen below 10 percent based on the 2010 official poverty threshold and became increasingly concentrated in remote areas in the western and central regions. For the remaining pockets of poor households, further poverty reduction was no longer driven by rising labor incomes but, instead, by the increasing role of private and public transfers (figure 2.2). Reallocation of employment out of agriculture and the growth of earnings among those in the bottom quintile slowed. As migration to urban areas accelerated, family transfers (remittances) became increasingly important to the relatively worse-off rural households at the end of the 2000s. Basic education fees were also waived for rural households beginning in the mid-2000s. Moreover, a new rural collective medical scheme was piloted in 2002 and scaled up in 2006.

Since 2009, the central government has strengthened social policy by extending the coverage of a basic noncontributory pension to rural areas and scaling up other social assistance transfers, which were complemented after 2012 by additional cash and in-kind support under the targeted poverty alleviation campaign. Consequently, public transfers became increasingly important in 2013–18 to lifting the most deprived out of poverty. The share of public transfers in total household income doubled (from 10 percent to 20 percent), driven by the increased coverage of rural pensions, the introduction of universal health care with a basic reimbursement package extended to rural areas, the expansion of social assistance, and social insurance and social assistance benefits (albeit benefit levels remained low).

China's demographic transition with falling dependency rates played a supporting role in poverty reduction over the entire period. Starting from an already relatively low birth rate, effective family planning interventions and the one-child policy introduced in 1982 (replaced in 2016 by a general two-child policy and in 2020 by a three-child policy), as well as improved health care, together led to a further reduction in the dependency rate (Naughton 2018). As birth rates declined, dependency rates fell sharply, increasing the share of working-age adults that could potentially contribute with increased labor income and thus drive poverty down. The share of the working-age population (ages 15–59) rose from 58.6 percent in 1982 to 70.1 percent in 2010, while the dependency ratio fell from 62.6 percent to 34.2 percent, as the share of children under age 15 fell from 33.6 percent to 16.6 percent and the total fertility rate remained well below two births per woman. After 2010, the trend reverted as the share of the elderly grew more rapidly than the rest of the population. According to the seventh national census data released in May 2021, the working-age population accounted for 63.3 percent of the total population in 2020, having dropped 6.7 percentage points, and the dependency ratio increased to 45.9 percent. Decomposition of poverty changes by income components suggests that changes in the share of the adult population (age 14 and above) contributed between 2 and 7 percentage points to poverty reduction throughout the decades (figure 2.2, panel a).

Notes

1. This chapter is based on chapter 1 of CIKD (forthcoming) and Lugo, Niu, and Yemtsov (2021).
2. Based on National Bureau of Statistics Yearbooks.
3. Income-based Gini index 1981–2001: Ravallion and Chen (2007) based on data provided by the National Bureau of Statistics of China (NBS), 2003–19: NBS Household Surveys Yearbook.
4. Whether high rates of economic growth could have been achieved without increases in inequality is not clear. Indeed, the same forces that drove development may well lie behind the increasing inequalities, creating incentives for some individuals and regions to invest more than others. Deng Xiaoping thus famously said, "let some people get rich first." Kuznets (1955) points to the likelihood that inequality would increase during the process of development. This report does not aim to resolve this point. Nonetheless, the decomposition in figure 2.1 is informative and shows that it was growth that drove poverty reduction up until 2010, while rising inequality mitigated its effect.
5. Semi-elasticity is defined as the percentage point reduction in poverty for every percentage point of economic growth. China's position in the ranking is similar if one considers semi-elasticities of mean income, or elasticities of per capita GDP or mean income.
6. World Bank (2009) studies economies that grew more than 7 percent per year for 25 years. China was among the 13 economies that shared that characteristic. Brazil, Indonesia, and South Africa (included in figure 2.1) were also in the group. But at least among those for which poverty data are available for a long period, and considering a longer time horizon, China is, indeed, an outlier.
7. See also Ravallion and Chen (2007) and Montalvo and Ravallion (2010).
8. Ravallion and Chen (2007) show that that during the 1980s and 1990s, coastal provinces had significantly higher rates of poverty reduction than inland provinces, even conditional on the initial level of poverty and inequality.

References

Azevedo, Joao Pedro, Gabriela Inchauste, Sergio Olivieri, Jaime Saavedra, and Hernan Winkler. 2013. "Is Labor Income Responsible for Poverty Reduction? A Decomposition Approach." Policy Research Working Paper 6414, World Bank, Washington, DC.

CIKD (Center for International Knowledge on Development). Forthcoming. *Economic Development and Poverty Alleviation in China*. Beijing: CIKD.

Datt, Gaurav, and Martin Ravallion. 1992. "Growth and Redistribution Components of Changes in Poverty Measures: A Decomposition with Applications to Brazil and India in the 1980s." *Journal of Development Economics* 38 (2): 275–95.

Fan, Shenggen, and Connic Chan-Kang. 2005. "Road Development, Economic Growth, and Poverty Reduction in China." Research Report 138, International Food Policy Research Institute, Washington, DC.

Fan, Shenggen, Ravi Kanbur, and Xiaobo Zhang. 2011. "China's Regional Disparities: Experience and Policy." *Review of Development Finance* 1 (1): 47–56.

Fan, Shenggen, Linxiu Zhang, and Xiaobo Zhang. 2004. "Reforms, Investment, and Poverty in Rural China." *Economic Development and Cultural Change* 52 (2): 395–421.

Kuznets, S. 1955. "Economic Growth and Income Inequality." *American Economic Review* 45 (1): 1–28.

Lugo, Maria Ana, Chiyu Niu, and Ruslan Yemtsov. 2021. "China's Poverty Reduction and Economic Transformation: A Decomposition Approach." Policy Research Working Paper 9849, World Bank, Washington, DC.

Montalvo, Jose G., and Martin Ravallion. 2010. "The Pattern of Growth and Poverty Reduction in China." *Journal of Comparative Economics* 38 (1): 2–16.

Naughton, Barry. 2018. *The Chinese Economy: Adaptation and Growth*. Second edition. Cambridge, MA: MIT Press.

Ravallion, Martin, and Shaohua Chen. 2007. "China's (Uneven) Progress against Poverty." *Journal of Development Economics* 82 (1): 1–42.

Riskin, Carl. 1987. *China's Political Economy: The Quest for Development since 1949.* Oxford, UK: Oxford University Press.

World Bank. 2009. *China—From Poor Areas to Poor People: China's Evolving Poverty Reduction Agenda—An Assessment of Poverty and Inequality.* Washington, DC: World Bank.

3

Drivers of China's Economic Transformation and Poverty Reduction

Introduction

All the standard elements of social and economic transformation are present in China: agricultural modernization, incremental industrialization, and progressive urbanization as well as domestic market integration thanks to expanding connectivity infrastructure. As in Lewis's canonical dual economy model, China's growth was driven by the reallocation of labor from the low-productivity ("traditional") agricultural sector to the higher-productivity ("modern") industrial sector (Lewis 1954). The country consistently created nonagricultural jobs, drawing on its labor abundance in rural areas and increased demand for goods and services in its cities as well as from the rest of the world. The process of economic transformation was facilitated by sound macroeconomic management and substantial public investment in connectivity infrastructure, which supported the competitiveness of industries and favored domestic market integration. Economic transformation coincided with a rapid demographic transition, which translated rising labor productivity into sharp increases in per capita incomes.

The drivers of economic growth shifted from agriculture to industry to services over time. In the two decades from 1980 to 2000, China's rapid economic growth was largely driven by growth in total factor productivity. The agricultural sector contributed less than 30 percent of overall gross domestic product (GDP) in 1978 but employed almost 70 percent of the labor force (figure 3.1). The reforms implemented under Deng Xiaoping's leadership resulted in huge efficiency gains in agriculture, which, in turn, made the reallocation of labor from agriculture to more productive industrial and service jobs possible and drove further gains in total factor productivity (Zhu 2012). Human and physical capital accumulation further supported and sustained the gains in income unleashed by the reform process.

After an initial explosion of growth in agriculture, with GDP growth peaking at 15 percent in 1983, the epicenter of growth moved to industry from about the mid-1980s to the mid-2010s. More recently, services have become the leading engine of growth. While total employment increased from 402 million in 1978 to 775 million in 2015, the share of agricultural labor dropped from 69.6 percent to 18.3 percent (Cai 2017).[1] The rise in employment occurred exclusively outside agriculture, fed by an expanding labor force. Services and manufacturing absorbed movers from agriculture and new entrants to the labor force, with a net job

FIGURE 3.1   **Rapid and sustained economic growth in China came about with fast economic transformation, 1978–2018**

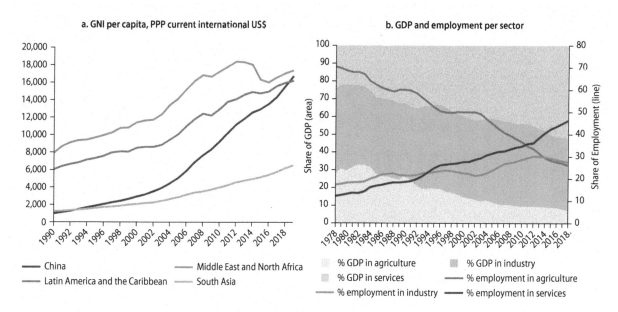

Sources: Merotto and Jiang 2021, based on World Development Indicators (panel a); National Bureau of Statistics of China 2020 (panel b).
Note: GDP = gross domestic product; GNI = gross national income; PPP = purchasing power parity.

creation rate close to 10 million per year (Li and Xing 2017). Cluster-based industrialization and export-oriented manufacturing in coastal regions fueled by high investment absorbed surplus rural labor nationwide through migration and urbanization (Long and Zhang 2011).

To understand how China's market-oriented reforms and the opening up of the economy could generate such a strong and sustained economic response, it is important to note that China benefited from a set of *initial conditions* that set the country apart from other transition economies in Eastern Europe and the former Soviet Union as well as other low-income countries in the developing world (Bardhan 2012; Nehru, Kraay, and Yu 1997; Ravallion 2009; Sachs and Woo 1994). Among others, these include the relatively low fertility rate, the widespread coverage of primary education, and the equal distribution of land.

Falling dependency ratios ensured that China's period of economic reform coincided with a rapid demographic transition, creating a large dividend, which contributed to poverty reduction as noted above. The reduction in birth rates in China started in the mid-1960s, following the adoption of family planning practices (such as the "Wan, Xi, Shao" [longer, later, fewer] campaign). The expansion of education for girls and the decline of infant mortality also contributed to the demographic transition (Harrell et al. 2011; Lavely and Freedman 1990). The fertility rate fell from 6.4 births per woman in 1965 to 2.9 by 1978.

For a country with a level of per capita income among the lowest in the world, China's population in 1978 had relatively high human capital endowments. In 1949, only 7 percent of those ages 15–64 had completed primary school in China.[2] Massive investment in education and expansion of health care since the 1950s resulted in real achievements: in 1978, the infant mortality rate was 52 per 1,000 births, less than half of the average in China's income group; life expectancy at birth at 66 years far exceeded that of other developing countries; the primary school enrollment rate was 96 percent; and the secondary school enrollment rate was 49.9 percent. The share of adults who had completed lower secondary education had tripled compared with 1949 to 22.8 percent (UNDP, China Institute for Development Planning at Tsinghua University, and State Information Center 2019). Human capital is widely recognized as a critical input for successful development (Bardhan 2012; Ravallion 2021).[3] China's strong endowments in this area allowed its population to rapidly benefit from new economic opportunities once market reforms set in (Bikales 2021).

Egalitarian land distribution also helped to spread the benefits of agricultural growth. From its planned economy period, China has inherited an equitable distribution of land: beginning in 1949, large-scale land reform was implemented, and more than 300 million landless peasants gained access to land.[4] Land was both a productive asset, the value of which shot up with the onset of reforms, and a safety net that helped households manage risks by cultivating their own garden plots (Naughton 2007). Indeed, it has been argued that the initial equal distribution of land played a key role in the success of poverty reduction in the early years of reform and opening up (for example, Ravallion and Chen 2007).[5]

In other words, China could be considered relatively poor in 1978 given its initial conditions, and thus the subsequent rapid pace of growth and poverty reduction reflected in part a process of catching up to the country's underlying economic opportunities. Alternatively, one could look at the process of poverty reduction since 1978 as the combined effect of the reforms introduced since then and the foundations laid in the decades before. This is important, because it helps put the sheer scale and speed of China's poverty reduction in perspective (Ravallion 2021). It does not lessen China's achievement.

The next sections present the main components of the economic transformation (growing agricultural productivity, progressive industrialization, and managed urbanization) supplemented by rapidly expanding infrastructure, focusing on the characteristics that made them inclusive. The aim is not to examine all the factors that drove this transformation, but to highlight some key reforms and policies underlying it. A detailed analysis of these reforms, their specific design, their political economy and thus replicability, and the lessons learned from China's experience in each of these areas is beyond the scope of this synthesis report.

Growing agricultural productivity: Higher incomes and more choices

Because China's poverty was concentrated in rural areas, in the first decades of reform, agricultural development was the main driver of poverty reduction in China.[6] According to some estimates, agriculture's contribution to the fall in poverty between 1978 and 2001 was four times that of industry or services (Ravallion 2009).[7] During this period, agricultural income per farmer improved across all income segments of the rural population (Lugo, Niu, and Yemtsov 2021). The rise in agricultural productivity contributed to poverty reduction through two main channels. First, higher productivity led to increased farmer incomes. Second, it released surplus labor to other sectors and urban areas. Thus, it allowed households to diversify income sources (and thereby reduce household risk) and to take advantage of better paid nonagricultural labor opportunities, locally and through migration.

Several factors lie behind the increases in agricultural productivity: the deepening of rural land reform, the liberalization of the output market and price systems, the gradual reduction of the tax burden and the shift to net agriculture subsidies, the massive investment in mechanization, irrigation and the use of modern inputs, and the marketization and integration of agricultural production into value chains. Considerable effort was also made to spur the development of agricultural research and extension and to better connect it to farming practices. These factors are unpacked below.

First, China's agricultural reforms started with land reform, which created incentives for farmers to increase production and use land more efficiently. Under the collective economic system in agriculture in place since 1953, land equitably distributed among farmer households was transferred to the collective, all inputs were provided by and all outputs were given to the collective. Agricultural adult workers were equally remunerated regardless of their actual contributions. Their incentives for production were consequently suppressed, resulting in long-term stagnation of agricultural productivity and widespread problems with food shortages. In late 1978, Anhui province piloted a new system whereby collectives would contract farm households to deliver a certain production quota from their allocated land, with the remaining output left for peasant households for their own consumption or to sell freely on the market. The success of this pilot led to the rapid nationwide adoption of the household responsibility system. By the end of 1983, about 94.2 percent of rural households were in the new system.

Studies show that between 1978 and 1984, the shift to the household responsibility system accounted for 30 percent to 50 percent of the total rise in agricultural output (Fan 1991; Gibson 2020; Huang and Rozelle 1996; Lin 1992). It contributed to rising agriculture factor productivity (Jin, Huang, and Rozelle 2002) and to a reduction in the gap between poorer and richer areas (Gibson 2020). To stabilize land contracting arrangements and to encourage investment in raising productivity, in 1984 the central government extended the contract duration from less than 3 years to 15 years, and then in 2002 further extended it to 30 years.[8] In 2011, the central government launched the land registration and certification system, allowing rural households to earn property income by subcontracting land to other farmers. The separation of land ownership rights, contracting rights, and management rights was piloted in 2014, creating conditions for entrepreneurial farmers and agricultural enterprises to develop large-scale operations through subleasing land from other entities, including in many cases migrant workers and elderly households no longer willing or able to farm themselves. In 2017, agricultural land rights were renewed for another 30 years, extending the duration of the original contracts to 75 years. The reform of land transfer rules has contributed to the emergence of "new-style" farms such as large family farms, cooperative farms, and farms run by agribusiness companies. To continue delivering expected outcomes, these reforms need to be complemented with investments in education and training and improved access to financial services.

Second, the gradual liberalization of the agricultural market and price system increased farmers' profits and reduced losses due to allocative inefficiency (Huang and Rozelle 2018). At the beginning of the period, farmers had to sell fixed quotas to the government at predefined low-level state procurement prices. After 1978, prices were gradually liberalized to encourage farmers to increase production. Initially introduced for major crops only, the dual-track system was based on a minimum production quota that was procured by the state at a fixed price, with the remaining output available for sale at the—much higher—market price. This, together with the household responsibility system, dramatically improved farmers' terms of trade and led to a sharp increase in agricultural output and incomes. Thus, from 1978 to 1995, the total procurement price index of agricultural products rose by 428.1 percent, far exceeding the 174.7 percent increase in the total retail price index of rural industrial products (National Bureau of Statistics of China 2001). As the scope for market pricing increased and the sale quotas were eliminated, allocative efficiency improved because farmers made decisions based on relative returns to their land and labor (de Brauw, Huang, and Rozelle 2004; Huang and Rozelle 1996). To protect the income of farmers affected by adverse movements in their terms of trade in the context of China's accession to the World Trade Organization (WTO) in 2001, the dual track pricing system gradually evolved into a "minimum price guarantee" for key products. Today, agricultural prices in general reflect market conditions, but input subsidies and price support mechanisms continue to play a significant role for key commodities.[9]

Third, government tax and aggregate support policies shifted in favor of agriculture. Traditionally, China's agricultural sector was a key source of taxation; this continued during the first decades after 1949, as the agricultural surplus was used to finance China's industrialization (Naughton 2018). However, after the initial surge in productivity following the 1978 reforms, the growth in rural incomes slowed and many farmers had insufficient profits to invest in badly needed modern technology and production methods. This situation led to a gradual shift in aggregate support policies: agriculture moved from being a net contributor to the budget up until the early 2000s to being a recipient of large net transfers (Anderson and Martin 2008). For example, in the 1990s, farmers' fiscal obligations to the state consisted of three village-level fees, four different agricultural taxes, and five township-level charges. These various outlays constituted a large burden, especially for poor farmers.[10] In 2006, China lifted all agricultural taxes, which had still accounted for about 5 percent to 7 percent of agricultural value added in the years before the reform (Naughton 2018; Song 2018). The abolition of agricultural taxes also meant that village committees no longer had own source revenues and had to rely on transfers from county and provincial governments. The provision and financing of services in rural areas is taken up again below.

Today China's agricultural support policies provide levels of support comparable to those in Organisation for Economic Co-operation and Development (OECD) countries, although they feature a relatively higher share of price support and input- or output-related measures. Since the late 2000s, China has also developed a series of transfer programs to poor rural communities that combine income support with payments for ecosystem services.[11] Such programs have the potential going forward to combine China's objective to sustain poverty reduction gains in rural areas with the goal of protecting China's natural wealth, generating triple economic, social, and environmental benefits (World Bank 2021).

Fourth, the modernization of China's agricultural sector was supported by substantial public investments in agricultural research, extension services, and production infrastructure. China's traditional agriculture was vulnerable to weather and natural disasters. Important investments thus included flood control projects, repairing field drainage ditches, improving soil structure, and reducing waterlogging. The use of plastic mulch film to conserve soil moisture, the wider application of chemical fertilizers and pesticides, and the use of agricultural machinery, as well as the development of better quality seeds, were key factors supporting higher yields.[12] The development of high-yield rice varieties in the 1970s, producing 20 percent to 30 percent more rice per acre, led to steeply rising harvests in China and across much of Asia and Africa.[13] Finally, the application of water-saving technologies such as sprinkler irrigation, microirrigation, and low-pressure pipe irrigation reduced water consumption per acre. The efficiency of irrigation increased from about half the OECD level in the 1970s to about three-quarters today.

Skills development and agricultural extension services supported farmers in adopting new technologies. By the mid-1980s, a public agricultural extension system had been built up at the county level. In 1993, the Agricultural Technology Extension Law laid the foundation for a gradual shift in the provision of extension services to market principles with a growing share of private actors in provision (OECD 2018). China's system of agricultural extension, using a combination of training, targets, and market-based incentives, has made a key contribution to agricultural modernization, overcoming farmers' risk aversion and greatly enhancing their understanding of modern agronomic practices (box 3.1).

Finally, the development of forward links to processing has been essential to increasing returns to agriculture. China has successively promulgated policies to encourage the industrialization of agriculture, the development of the agro-processing industry, and the integration of rural primary, secondary, and tertiary industries. Local governments set up specialized agricultural wholesale markets, and farmers were encouraged to form cooperatives to share the cost of mechanized inputs as well as invest in processing, storage, quality control, and marketing facilities. By the end of 2016, 53 percent of farmer cooperatives had developed their own processing and marketing facilities. The processing rate of agricultural products at the cooperative or farm level reached 65 percent, generating an increase of 2.2 times in the value added retained at the farm. Since 2014, the Chinese government has issued a series of policies to promote the development of rural e-commerce, supporting logistics, commerce, and finance of agriculture-related e-commerce, carrying out comprehensive demonstrations of e-commerce in rural areas, and encouraging the development of rural markets (Luo and Niu 2019).

BOX 3.1 Agricultural technology extension for poverty reduction: Promoting mulch film in Guyuan

Guyuan County is located in Mount Liupan, a poverty-stricken area in the Ningxia Hui Autonomous Region of China. It is widely known as Xihaigu, where harsh natural conditions stemming from limited water and barren land had caused low crop yields of less than 50 kilograms per acre and large-scale severe famines even 30 years after the founding of the People's Republic of China.

The government started to research film-mulching technology applications in Xihaigu in the early 1980s. The technology was intended to maintain favorable soil temperature early in the season, retain moisture, and help in collecting precipitation. The government of Guyuan dispatched agricultural extension workers (or technicians) to conduct experiments with film-mulching corn planting in villages. Technicians provided free seeds, mulch films, and other inputs, while peasants offered their labor and land, earning all output and additional daily labor income. This early experiment confirmed that mulch films could increase outputs.

Under the Strategy of Science and Technology for Agriculture in 1985, Guyuan established a Science and Technology for Agriculture Development Leading Group, which prioritized the supply of mulch films for agriculture and encouraged and supported extension workers and demonstration households. Importantly, the government assigned to the township extension stations the political task of demonstration sites. Because this became part of their performance

assessment, officials held frequent village meetings to encourage villagers to use the mulch film. However, only a few households were interested in utilizing this technique because it was labor consuming given the rugged terrain characteristic of the county. To overcome the lack of interest, executive measures were taken to assign land for the use of the new technology. As a result, the target of planting 400 acres of corn with mulch films was achieved in Guyuan in 1987 and corn yields increased by 30 percent.

In the 1990s, farmers began to use cattle and other draft animals to apply mulch films. Gradually, farmers invented small mechanical tools that cost less than 100 yuan. These methods were later replaced by walking tractors, increasing the efficiency of film spreading from three people for 1 mu (about 0.16 acre) per day to five people for 20 mu per day. In 2000, Guyuan County raised 430,000 yuan and purchased 623 special film-mulching planters.

In the mid-1990s, the Food and Clothing Project in Guyuan created a contract responsibility system to further support the use of mulch film. It allocated projects and tasks to technicians and government officials. The technicians in intermediate and junior positions were personally responsible for 300 mu and 200 mu of demonstration sites per person, respectively, and the township-level leaders and general officials were personally responsible for 50 mu and 30 mu of demonstration sites, respectively.

Source: CIKD case study on mulch films extension in Guyuan, carried out by CIKD team (World Bank, forthcoming).

Progressive industrialization: Better jobs for more people

China's industrialization was key to the country's long-term success in growth and poverty reduction.[14] From 1978 to 2020, China's industrial value added increased at an average annual real rate of 10.3 percent.[15] More and better job opportunities became available. With a massive supply of cheap agricultural surplus labor as well as an improving business environment, China became a competitive investment destination on a global scale.[16] In the early stages of economic reform, rural urban labor flows were tightly managed, restricting access of migrants to urban services as well as social security. This kept labor costs low and limited additional spending pressures on cities to accommodate migrant worker families, while nonetheless offering more migrant workers significantly higher incomes than what they earned in their home villages. On the other hand, it slowed the rapid integration of migrants into the urban labor force—a duality that persists to the present day.[17] Increased earnings and investment in the "modern sector" in China's cities generated new demand for consumer goods and services, in turn encouraging additional investment and creating new jobs.

Since the mid-1990s, the biggest gains in per capita income growth have come from labor productivity increases *within* sectors, especially from industry. Compared with the other fastest growing developing economies in the world over the period 1995–2018, China stands out by the large contribution (over 5.4 percentage points) of within-sector labor productivity to total per capita growth, with over half coming from industry (figure 3.2). Structural change (meaning shifts across sectors) added 1.8 percentage points to per capita income growth in China, matching the contribution of structural change in poorer Bangladesh and India. Fast labor productivity growth was driven by strong capital accumulation, financed by a combination of corporate profits and household savings.

A key feature of China's industrialization strategy from the 1980s onward was its export orientation. During the 1950s through the 1970s, China prioritized heavy industry and national security and had very limited interaction with the world economy. The market-oriented reforms introduced at the beginning of the 1980s aimed at capitalizing on China's comparative advantage in more labor-intensive light industry, using export demand as a driver for investment and special economic zones in coastal areas as a platform for attracting foreign investment and technology. The country's total exports of goods in 2018 reached 16.4 trillion yuan (US$2.49 trillion), and manufactured exports rose from 46.5 percent of the total in 1978 to 96 percent (National Bureau of Statistics of China 2020).

FIGURE 3.2 Labor productivity, particularly from industry, drove high economic growth, 1995–2018

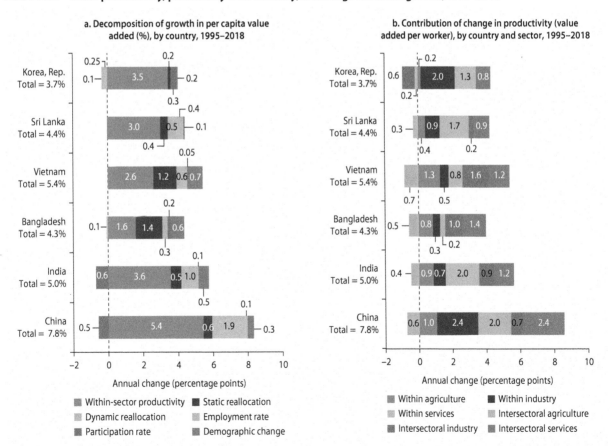

Source: Merotto and Jiang 2021, based on World Development Indicators and Chinese Household Income Project survey.

Export demand was only one of the drivers of industrialization, however. During the initial reform period, significant industrial job creation occurred in rural areas, using highly labor-intensive technologies and producing goods in short supply in the domestic market. From 1978 to the mid-1990s, emerging township and village enterprises (TVEs) absorbed a large number of rural workers no longer required on the farm as agricultural productivity increased. The number of TVEs surged from 1.5 million in 1978 to 23 million in 1996, most of them engaged in light industry. Throughout this period, TVEs generated more than 130 million jobs, and their contribution to rural employment increased from 9.2 percent to 27.6 percent (Gan 2003) (figure 3.3). The expansion of alternative rural employment opportunities was a critical element of China's rapid rural poverty reduction during the first two decades of reform and opening up.

The reasons for this explosion in entrepreneurial activity through TVEs are manifold. For poor agricultural workers, jobs in TVEs were attractive because they did not require them to leave their villages and household plots. This allowed risk-averse farmers to complement farm incomes with wages from off-farm employment during times when their labor was not needed on the farm (Huang 1985). Local governments had strong incentives to develop a production base because additional tax revenues could largely be retained at the local level and the unmet demand for consumer goods provided a ready outlet for rural production (Naughton 2018). Local government officials in some locations responded to these opportunities by becoming entrepreneurs themselves, using their favorable access to factors of production, including labor and land (Lin, Cai, and Li 2003),[18] and countering the lack of secure private property rights by using flexible risk-sharing arrangements, adapted to local conditions (Cai, Wang, and Du 2002; Fan and Chan-Kang 2005). The presence of well-educated youth, "sent down" to the countryside during the Cultural Revolution, arguably also contributed to allowing ostensibly backward rural areas to rapidly seize new economic opportunities (Bikales 2021).

In the second half of the 1990s, in preparation for WTO accession, export-oriented industries in coastal areas and TVEs gradually integrated. As coastal areas thrived, supply chains were extended further inland, driving additional investment and modernization. Following a wave of privatization, many TVEs and nonessential state-owned enterprises became private

FIGURE 3.3   Employment and productivity of manufacturing, 1978–2001

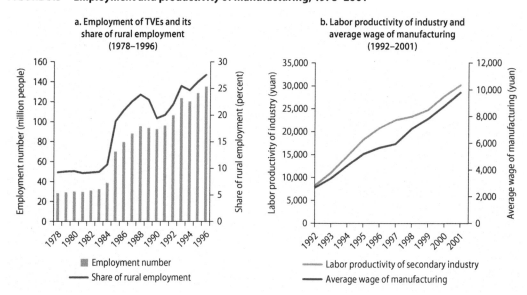

a. Employment of TVEs and its share of rural employment (1978–1996)

b. Labor productivity of industry and average wage of manufacturing (1992–2001)

- Employment number
- Share of rural employment
- Labor productivity of secondary industry
- Average wage of manufacturing

Sources: Chapter 3 of CIKD (forthcoming) based on Gan 2003 (panel a); Statistical Department of Industry and Communication, National Bureau of Statistics of China 2002 (panel b).
Note: TVEs = township and rural enterprises.

companies, some counted among China's leading industrial enterprises today. By 2005, collective firms represented only a tiny proportion of employment in TVEs (Naughton 2018).

While China's industrialization strategy was initially based on cheap labor, with labor productivity increasing more rapidly than earnings, increasing investment in physical and human capital allowed China to move up the value chain in a growing number of sectors.[19] Alongside improvements in education access, a significant public health effort helped make the labor force healthier and more productive.[20] Through "learning by doing" and vocational training, some rural migrants who had received little formal schooling beyond compulsory levels were equipped with skills that allowed them to become more productive and increase their income (see box 3.2 on the valve making industry). From 1992 to 2001, the average labor productivity of secondary industry increased from 8,150 yuan to 30,133 yuan and the average annual manufacturing wage tripled from 2,635 yuan to 9,774 yuan (figure 3.3).

China's WTO accession in 2001 significantly accelerated the process of industrial upgrading, turning China into a giant workshop for the global economy. The share of foreign trade in China's GDP rose significantly, from 39.6 percent in 2000 to 63.8 percent in 2005. In 2009, China's export value reached US$1.2 trillion and it replaced Germany as the largest global exporter. Chen and Ravallion (2004); Hertel, Zhai, and Wang (2004); and Sicular and Zhao (2004) present evidence of the positive impact of China's WTO accession on average household incomes. Although the resulting terms of trade shifts benefited predominantly urban consumers, rural households nonetheless benefited indirectly through new job opportunities and through the remittances from migrant workers, and were additionally supported by the shift in net government taxation of the agricultural sector as discussed in the previous section (Anderson and Martin 2008).

Shortly after WTO accession, China began to adopt national strategies aimed at closing regional disparities that had widened in the previous decade. Regional development strategies such as the Western Development Program and the Rise of Central China promoted industrial investment in these regions, channeling government resources to improve connectivity with the eastern region and the global production system. The composition of total investment in fixed assets shifted away from the eastern region, with its share declining from 66 percent in 2003

BOX 3.2   Upgrading skills through learning by doing: How Mr. Xie Dewu set up his own valve-making company in Yongjia

Valve making is one of the pillar industries in Yongjia, populated by about 400 small and medium enterprises. Henghua Safety Valve Company with 80 employees ranked in the top 150 of these firms by sales. It manufactures products with high safety requirements for the electric and petroleum industries. Its boss, Mr. Xie Dewu, was born into a poor family and rose to be an entrepreneur through learning by doing. After graduating from lower secondary school, Xie worked for five years with his elder brother in processing spare valve parts in a family workshop. In his daily work, with the help of family and friends, he gradually learned the ropes in opera-

tions, enriched his technical knowledge, expanded his social network, and accumulated capital. In 2008, he set up his company, Henghua, which in 2018 generated output worth 40 million yuan a year, led by substantial progress in competitiveness and technology adoption. Now, Henghua is upgrading its workshops with digital and automation technology.

Among the five enterprises the Center for International Knowledge on Development team visited in Yongjia, the owners of three of them, including Mr. Xie, had completed only lower secondary school. Their human capital is accumulated through learning by doing.

Source: CIKD case study on poverty alleviation in Yongjia, carried out by the CIKD team (World Bank, forthcoming).

to 43 percent by 2012, and the share going to the western and central regions correspondingly increasing. High commodity prices and lower wages fueled investment in the manufacturing and natural resource sectors in interior provinces, as wages and land prices rose rapidly in coastal areas. The result of these efforts was a gradual decline in the income gap between the coast and the interior, although it remains large compared with the United States or the European Union (World Bank 2020).

As industrialization deepened in the decades following WTO accession, Chinese workers benefited from more and better paid job opportunities. The number of employees in secondary industry grew from 157 million in 2002 to a peak of 232 million in 2012, as the share in total employment rose from 21.4 percent to 30.3 percent (National Bureau of Statistics of China 2020). The rapid industrialization brought younger workers of all skill levels to cities. With the urban transformation came the diversification of jobs into industry (figure 3.4), especially construction (primarily among male youth), and into services (particularly among women). Wage employment expanded from 45 percent of total employment in 1988 to 73 percent in 2013 (figure 3.4), with over 200 million additional wage jobs. The shift into wage employment was accompanied by the growth of the private formal sector, particularly among the better-educated workers.

Accompanying the process of industrial upgrading was a sharp increase in the educational attainment of the labor force. Between 1988 and 2013, the share of workers with at least complete secondary schooling increased 3.8 percent per year. This was a result of deliberate education policy, gradually shifting from prioritizing universal access to primary education to increasing emphasis on extending compulsory schooling (in the late 1990s), providing marketable skills training and education quality. The accumulation of human capital, through formal schooling and learning by doing, thus contributed to fast labor productivity growth.

The creation of higher-paying waged jobs, the expansion of educational attainment, and broad-based wage growth have helped narrow the rural-urban earnings gap since the early 2000s. Mean and median wages grew throughout the period. From 2002 to 2013, real median

FIGURE 3.4 **Workers benefited from the diversification of jobs and the expansion of wage employment, 1998–2013**

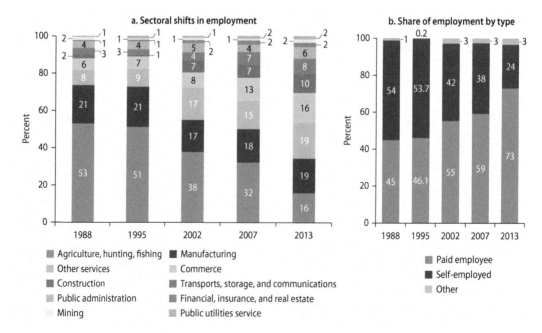

Source: Merotto and Jiang 2021, based on Chinese Household Income Project survey.

monthly wages more than tripled, rising faster than the average monthly wage.[21] Wages remained higher in urban than in rural areas, but rural-to-urban migration dampened the real increase in labor costs to urban firms and narrowed rural-urban wage gaps (figure 3.5). The creation of urban and eventually rural waged jobs in processing industries and services also tightened rural labor markets and consequently increased the labor returns to poorer rural workers. This evidence is consistent with the idea that China may have reached the "Lewis tipping point" in or around 2007, as several authors have noted using alternative data sources (see, for instance, Cai and Du 2011; Kanbur, Wang, and Zhang 2021; Zhang, Yang, and Wang 2011).[22]

China's industrial upgrading will continue, but industry's contribution to providing better opportunities to a growing number of people is unlikely to be sustained. Going forward, the service sector will need to take

FIGURE 3.5   **Wage gaps between urban and rural areas narrowed, suggesting that China reached the Lewis tipping point around 2007**

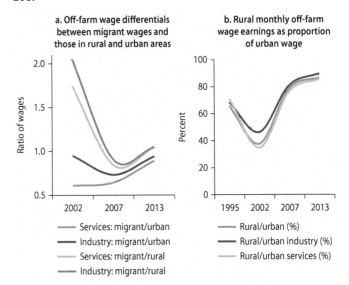

Source: Merotto and Jiang 2021, based on Chinese Household Income Project survey.

the leading role in net job creation. Manufacturing employment in China reached a peak of 148 million in 2013 and then fell by 8.5 million in the following four years (Zhuo and Huang 2019). At the same time, from 2013 to 2019, the proportion of migrant workers employed in the service sectors increased to 51 percent. As discussed in the next section, remittances from migrant workers in urban areas have played an important role in poverty reduction in recent years.

Managed urbanization: Multiple gains for migrants and nonmigrant rural families, but persistent inequality of opportunities

Along with industrial growth, the rapid urbanization of China's population was another key driver of economic transformation and poverty reduction.[23] As depicted by the Lewis model, new opportunities were generated outside agriculture, attracting rural workers to urban areas and increasing the share of the urban population. Urbanization contributed to poverty reduction directly by improving the livelihoods and increasing the earnings of migrants, and indirectly by reducing poverty among the nonmigrants in rural areas. This section summarizes the findings on these two fronts.

Rapid economic development in China was accompanied by the fast urbanization of its population. The urban population has more than quadrupled from about 200 million in 1980 to 900 million in 2020, representing an increase in the urbanization rate from 19.4 percent in 1980 to 63.9 percent in 2020 (National Bureau of Statistics of China 2021). Cities that today have 10 million inhabitants or more, such as Shenzhen, Foshan, and Dongguan, were very small or did not even exist in the 1980s (Hamnett 2020). Although China's pace of urbanization was fast, the pattern of urbanization and growth is similar to that of other countries (figure 3.6, panel a), particularly those that went through comparable processes of fast economic transformation, such as India and Vietnam (figure 3.6, panel b) (see also World Bank and DRC 2014). Given its level of development, the urban share of China's population is lower than expected. Continued urbanization could be a key factor in sustaining growth into the next decade (Huang 2017; World Bank and DRC 2019).

FIGURE 3.6   **Urbanization in China followed a similar pattern as other fast-growing economies, 1960–2019**

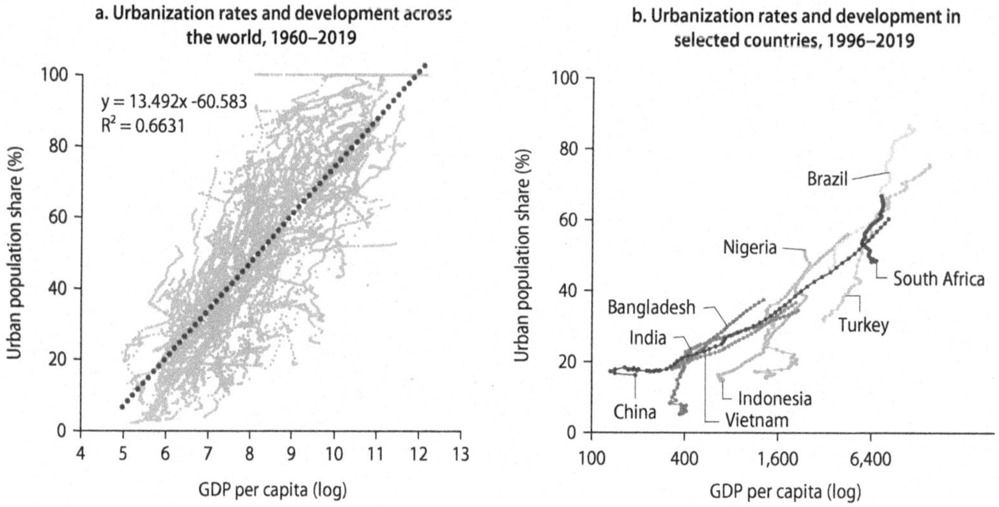

a. Urbanization rates and development across the world, 1960–2019

b. Urbanization rates and development in selected countries, 1996–2019

Source: World Development Indicators, World Bank.
Note: GDP = gross domestic product.

Urbanization does not automatically lead to economic growth, as the experience in some African and Latin American countries shows (Gollin, Jedwab, and Vollrath 2016; Rodrik 2016).[24] The association of urbanization with rapid growth and poverty reduction in China was therefore not a foregone conclusion. For example, using cross-country data from 1993 to 2002, and accounting for cost-of-living differences between urban and rural areas, Raval-lion, Chen, and Sangraula (2007) find that urban poverty increased in Latin America and in Sub-Saharan Africa at a time when poverty in rural areas was declining and the regions were urbanizing. By contrast, in China estimates suggest that urban poverty remained well below 3 percent for most of the period (Chen and Ravallion 2021; Ravallion and Chen 2007). China has also expanded economic opportunities in urban areas much faster than other economies have (as discussed in the next section), which was key to the rapid growth of real wages. But institutional factors have also played a role.

The pattern of urbanization in China has been determined by specific policies that limited the growth of its megacities. The key policy instrument in this regard is the *hukou*, an administrative tool for population movement. A hukou determines a person's residence permit, grants its holder the legal right to live and work in a particular location, and regulates access to key government services, such as social security and public education.[25] Jointly with the land tenure system, the hukou system has shaped migration patterns, migration duration, and the demographic composition of migrants. Proponents of the hukou argue that it played an important role in preventing the urbanization of poverty through the uncontrolled growth of urban slums. On the other hand, critics of the hukou point out that it cemented inequities in access to key government services, which reduced intergenerational social mobility over time (Bikales 2021; Hell and Rozelle 2020). This study will not resolve this debate, which is ongoing within China, even as the hukou restrictions on migration to most cities, with the exception of the largest coastal cities, have been progressively relaxed. We simply lack a counterfactual to determine what would have happened in the absence of hukou restrictions. What can be concluded is that the migration from rural to urban areas on the whole contributed to poverty reduction. How this occurred is summarized below.

Rural to urban migration began in the 1980s but accelerated sharply in the 2000s, facilitated by a gradual relaxation of mobility restrictions. Population movements between rural and urban areas began to increase in the 1980s with the emergence of the market economy, driven by increased labor demand, very large wage differentials between new urban growth centers and rural areas, and the consequent adoption of more flexible hukou policies.[26] Since then, rural-to-urban migration has continuously risen over the years (figure 3.7, panel a). By 2000, more than half (51.1 percent) of poor families had members commuting as migrant workers (Zhu and He 2018).

While many first migration experiences were to urban areas within home provinces, the demand for labor in coastal regions—following the establishment of special economic zones—progressively induced migrants to leave their home provinces. After the mid-1990s, private local businesses also became important sources of migrant employment (Chen and Coulson 2002). Since 2000, the Western Development Program and the relocation of labor-intensive industries westward offered more opportunities for employment in the inland regions, reducing migration to the coastal cities and increasing intraprovincial flow (figure 3.7, panel a). According to the 7th China National Population Census (2020), more than 66 percent of the "floating population" (those living for at least six months in a place different from their hukou registration) moved within their home provinces.[27] By 2018, the total number of migrant workers topped 288 million,[28] with migrant workers from rural areas accounting for over 40 percent of total urban employment.

The migration of workers from rural to urban areas reduced poverty, both directly by helping migrant workers increase their wage earnings, and indirectly through the transfer of remittances to rural households with one or several migrant worker members. Earnings of migrants rose steadily over the years and accelerated beginning in the mid-2000s. Average incomes of the "floating population" quadrupled from 2005 to 2019 (figure 3.8). Even if the income gains achieved by moving to the cities were significant,[29] migrants initially earned far less than urban resident workers. However, in recent years, as the pool of surplus agricultural labor has declined, the wage gaps between migrant workers and urban residents started to decline.[30]

FIGURE 3.7 **Migration has increased consistently over time, as have migrant earnings as a share of total household income, 1993–2017**

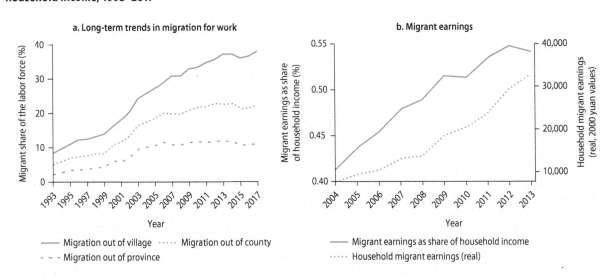

Source: Giles and Mu 2022, based on Annual Village Surveys from the Ministry of Agriculture, Research Center for Rural Economy Fixed Point Survey. See appendix A for more information on the survey.

FIGURE 3.8   "Floating" populations' income per month

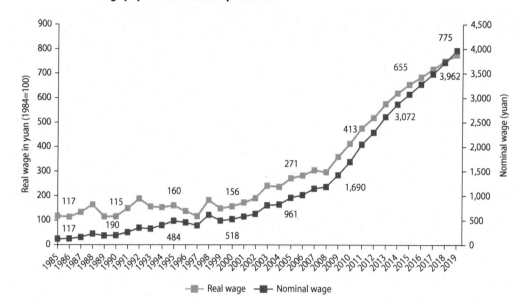

Source: CIKD (forthcoming), chapter 4, based on Lu 2012.
Note: Nominal wage from 2013 to 2019 is based on the NBS "Migrant Workers Monitoring Survey Report" and is converted to real wage with the consumer price index. "Floating" population is defined as those migrants who have moved across a township-level boundary for more than six months without changing their places of household registration.

Guo, Tan, and Qu (2018) show that by 2015, income poverty rates among migrant workers in urban areas were fairly low.[31]

The second important way in which migration contributed to poverty reduction is indirectly, through the contribution to rural household incomes. Data from an annual survey in rural villages carried out by the Ministry of Agriculture indicate that the share of migrant earnings in total rural household incomes increased from about 40 percent in 2004 to 55 percent in 2012 (figure 3.7, panel b).

Given that the more able workers are more likely to migrate, estimates of the impact of migrant earnings on poverty need to be corrected for selection effects. Using such a correction, Du, Park, and Wang (2005) find that households with migrants have per capita incomes 8.5 percent to 13.1 percent higher than those without migrants. At the village level, based on data between 1995 and 2002, a 1 percentage point increase in village out-migration is associated with a 10 percent increase in consumption by poor households (de Brauw and Giles 2018). This finding suggests that migrant earnings contribute to village prosperity, for instance, by increasing demand for nonagricultural activities. Indeed, de Brauw and Giles (2018) find that more affluent households tended to increase their labor supply in local nonagricultural activities, thus benefiting more from out-migration than less affluent households, who instead opted to reduce agricultural labor supply and spent more days working outside the home township.

In addition to boosting household incomes through transfers, out-migration also reduced poverty among rural households by encouraging greater risk-taking and offering insurance against negative income shocks. As households diversified income sources, consumption variability declined, and investment in higher-risk, more productive activities increased (Kinnan, Wang, and Wang 2018). A 1 percentage point increase in the share of a village workforce employed as migrants is associated with a 3.2 percentage point decline in the probability of falling into poverty, and among the poor, the same increase in migration is associated with a 3.5 percentage point reduction in the probability of remaining poor (Giles and Murtazashvili 2013).

Although a powerful force in boosting living standards of the rural poor, migration also had some negative social consequences, potentially widening inequalities. As China becomes more and more urbanized, overcoming these inequalities will be a key challenge for future social policies. First, many rural migrants work in low-wage sectors, often in informal jobs that leave them vulnerable to shocks. Moreover, Guo, Tan, and Qu (2018) find that although income poverty of migrant workers was low, their consumption poverty was significant, given that many saved part of their incomes to send to their families in rural areas. Indeed, former migrant workers that have permanently settled in cities consume up to 30 percent more than those without urban hukou (Molnar, Chalaux, and Ren 2017). Migrant workers in urban areas also suffered from poor housing conditions (particularly sanitation) and lack of access to health care (Guo, Tan, and Qu 2018). These are challenges migrant and informal workers share with their peers in many other developing countries (World Bank and DRC 2014).[32] They are outweighed in China's case by the substantial income gains migrant workers experienced (CIKD, forthcoming). But they set a new agenda for China's social policies going forward.

Second, even after the relaxation of hukou rules, migrants did not gain full access to urban social services (for example, urban education and health care) and social benefits (such as housing subsidies, unemployment benefits, disability benefits, and various old-age benefits). Not until 2014 was a single national resident registration system set up.[33] This reform differentiated between large and small-to-medium-sized cities and encouraged rural migrants to settle down in small and medium-sized cities, giving them full access to services and social rights. Implementation of this reform is incomplete, because local governments often lack the resources to grant migrant workers full residency rights, and urban enterprises are reluctant to shoulder the additional costs that would come with granting migrants formal urban employment status. As documented in Giles et al. (2021) using the Rural-Urban Migration in China longitudinal survey,[34] in 2016, 68 percent of migrants were still employed in the informal sector, and fewer than 20 percent were enrolled in urban health and social security schemes.[35] Of those migrants employed as formal sector workers, on the other hand, over 80 percent were covered by urban pension and health insurance.

Finally, some studies have identified a *positive* relationship between parental migration and child health and learning outcomes, likely reflecting the income effects of migration.[36] In contrast, studies that focus on children's mental health, behavioral issues, and delinquency consistently conclude that the impact of parental out-migration is unambiguously negative (Guang et al. 2017; Tang et al. 2018).[37] The negative impact suggests that decline in time with parents dominates the income effect. These studies conclude that reduced parental supervision and protection and weakened parent-child bonding and communication resulting from parental migration cannot be compensated for through increased economic resources gained by migrant employment.[38] A similar mixed pattern is seen for the welfare of left-behind elderly.[39] With rising income levels, the nonmaterial dimensions of deprivation tend to take a greater role in influencing overall perceptions of well-being.

Expanded infrastructure investment: Improved connectivity and job creation for the poor

At the onset of reforms, China's initial conditions for infrastructure, especially transport infrastructure, suggested a significant disadvantage.[40,41] Sustained public investment in infrastructure was thus an important factor in China's economic growth and poverty reduction story (Chatterjee 2005; Straub 2008). Arguably, it was particularly important as a catalyst for China's domestic market integration, providing the poor with improved access to markets to sell their produce and for their own consumption needs, and allowing the gains from China's export-led development and managed urbanization to be shared with the interior provinces and with rural areas.

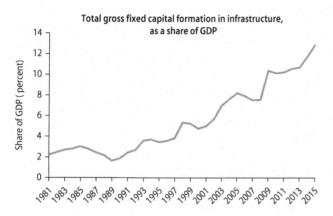

Total gross fixed capital formation in infrastructure, as a share of GDP

Source: Herd 2020.
Note: GDP = gross domestic product.

Infrastructure investment was a key factor in supporting China's rapid growth. Industrial development and urbanization dramatically increased the demand for energy, water, and industrial land. Without corresponding increases in infrastructure investment China's growth would have rapidly run into physical constraints. Although investment in infrastructure was relatively limited during the 1980s, it picked up beginning in 1990 and has risen sharply since the global financial crisis, when the authorities used public investment (primarily financed by off-budget financing channels) to stimulate growth (Herd 2020) (figure 3.9). Numerous cross-country studies have established a causal relationship between economic growth and a minimum amount of infrastructure investment.[42] However, this literature also shows that the relationship is not linear, and above a certain level, the amount of public investment in infrastructure is ultimately a function of the service quality a government wishes to provide and the willingness and ability of users to pay for it—either through taxes or user fees.

China's approach to infrastructure investment has emphasized high service coverage, while using a combination of general government transfers and local land development auctions as a means of financing. Tariffs cover capital and operational costs in the energy sector, albeit with significant cross-subsidies from industry to households (World Bank 2020; World Bank and DRC 2014), but capital costs (and sometimes operational costs) are generally not recovered in the other infrastructure sectors (transport, water, and other municipal services).[43] This approach to infrastructure financing, put in place following the fiscal recentralization of the early 1990s, worked well until the early 2010s. In the aftermath of the global financial crisis, to which China reacted with a large debt-financed infrastructure push, concerns over its sustainability have grown. Today, China's public capital stock per worker (largely made up of infrastructure assets) corresponds to the level in the OECD, even though the country's per capita GDP is only a fifth of the OECD average (World Bank and DRC 2019). The contribution of traditional infrastructure investment to economic growth is thus unlikely to continue going forward. New infrastructure investments in fields such as digital technology, clean energy, and intracity transport will to some extent replace the role of traditional connectivity infrastructure as a driver of future growth, but more sustainable financing models and an overall rebalancing toward consumption will also be needed. The remainder of this section focuses on the contribution of rural infrastructure investments to poverty reduction through improved connectivity, market integration, and job creation.

The impact of infrastructure on poverty reduction worked along several pathways. First, it greatly facilitated and sometimes catalyzed the establishment and development of competitive businesses in inland and rural areas. Second, infrastructure construction and maintenance, being a labor-intensive industry, generated demand for relatively low-skilled labor. In some of the government's poverty reduction interventions the two went hand in hand, such as when public investments in the construction of rural roads or irrigation infrastructure were designed to benefit local low-skilled workers by incorporating local employment requirements in bidding documents. Finally, infrastructure investment in safe water, connectivity, and energy, particularly in poor areas, directly improved poor families' access to basic services, and thus improved their well-being.

In the early reform period, heavy investments in intercity expressways were a major force in China's economic transformation, particularly in the coastal areas (Hajj and Pendakur 2000).

The total length of expressways increased from 147 kilometers in 1988 to 25,130 kilometers in 2002,[44] equivalent to an average annual growth rate of 44 percent. In contrast, the length of low-quality, mostly rural roads increased by only 3 percent per year over the same period (Fan and Chan-Kang 2005). Since 1994 and the adoption of the 8–7 Poverty Eradication plan (see chapter 4), more attention has been paid to improving connectivity in rural areas.

There is clear evidence of the positive contribution of connectivity investments, particularly in rural roads, to agricultural and nonagricultural output growth in rural areas (Fan and Chan-Kang 2005).[45] This is in line with international evidence (Jacoby 2002). Fan and Chang-Kang (2005) present upper bound estimates of the effect of public infrastructure investment on poverty: in the mid-1990s, every 10,000 yuan of public spending on roads may have moved 3 people out of poverty, compared with 2 people for the same spending on access to electricity and telecommunications and 1 person in the case of irrigation. These effects were much larger in the western region (10 people moved out of poverty for each 10,000 yuan spent on rural roads) than in other parts of rural China. Other studies confirm the positive spillover effects of infrastructure investments on rural growth for later periods (Yu et al. 2013).

Beyond the role of infrastructure as a foundation of economic transformation, it also expanded job opportunities for rural low-skilled workers. Most construction workers were local rural residents or migrants from rural areas. The importance of construction as the second major source of employment for migrant workers increased over time, from 15.2 percent of the migrant workforce in 1997[46] to 22.3 in 2013 before declining to 18 percent in 2019. Employment in construction was also lucrative: by 2019, the monthly salary of migrant workers in the construction industry rose to 4,567 yuan, 15.3 percent higher than the average level among migrants.

In addition, infrastructure became an instrument of targeted regional development and sometimes direct poverty reduction. Public works and bidding rules favoring local employment creation were part of these targeted policies. Thus, between 20 percent and 30 percent of the total funds allocated to support underdeveloped or poverty-stricken areas was spent on rural infrastructure.[47] Public works projects were targeted to poor areas to provide direct employment opportunities for poor families. These projects used participatory mechanisms to include communities in planning, management, and the maintenance of assets. They were specifically designed to attract the rural poor, and their performance indicators included salaries paid to workers. Zhu and Jiang (2004) study these programs in two rural counties in Shaanxi and Sichuan, and Zhu (1997) provides an initial aggregate account confirming the positive impact on poverty.

Finally, infrastructure played a direct role in reducing multidimensional poverty. Indeed, access to basic infrastructure was included as a criterion for counties and villages to exit the list of poverty-stricken areas, which provided local governments with incentives to invest in infrastructure (see more discussion in box 4.2). Using data from the China Health and Nutrition Survey, Qi and Wu (2016) show that better access to improved water, sanitation, and shelter significantly contributed to the reduction of multidimensional poverty among children between 1989 and 2009, which fell from 64 percent to 19 percent over this period. According to the UNDP's Multidimensional Poverty Index, from 2010 to 2014, there were 70 million fewer multidimensional poor people in China, as the multidimensional poverty rate dropped from 9.5 percent to 4.2 percent. Among the multidimensional poor, the share of the people deprived of sanitation dropped from 4.4 percent to 1 percent and of drinking water from 7.2 percent to 2.1 percent, while none of them lacked access to electricity (UNDP and OPHI 2020).

Notes

1. Note that different sources of data (Labor Force Surveys versus Population Census data) point to different estimates of total employment, while trends are broadly consistent across sources.
2. Barro-Lee database, http://www.barrolee.com/.

3. See also Human Capital Project, https://www.worldbank.org/en/publication/human-capital.

4. After the 1949 land reform, China initiated the people's commune system (Renmin Gongshe Yundong) in 1953, which transferred the land from peasants to the commune. With the 1978 reform, land was again distributed to each household equally.

5. This is also related to the evidence by Deininger and Squire (1998) based on cross-country analysis, which concludes that land inequality has a negative effect on economic growth.

6. Based on CIKD (forthcoming), chapter 2. The literature on China's agricultural reforms is vast and no attempt is made here to provide a comprehensive summary. For a good overview of the evidence, see Naughton (2018) and Huang and Rozelle (2018). For earlier analysis of China's agricultural reforms, see World Bank (1997).

7. Ravallion and Chen (2007) and Montalvo and Ravallion (2010) estimate that in the 1980s and 1990s, agriculture was "the real driving force in China's remarkable success against absolute poverty, rather than the secondary (manufacturing) or tertiary (services) sectors" (Montalvo and Ravallion 2010, 13). On the importance of agriculture for poverty reduction, see also World Bank Poverty Assessments (1992, 2001, 2009).

8. Although long-term leases encouraged farmers to invest in measures to increase yields, incentives to invest in maintaining the long-term value of the land were low until recent reforms creating transferable land leases. This will be important in the context of shifting to more environmentally sustainable production practices and reducing excess use of fertilizers and pesticides.

9. The minimum price guarantee has been applied to rice and wheat and on an irregular basis to some other agricultural products such as soybeans and cotton. The state-owned China Grain Reserves Corporation (Sinograin) and other state-owned companies used to purchase these key products at the minimum purchase price if the market price fell below a minimum price. In 2014, China began piloting a new target price system for selected agricultural products such as soybeans and cotton in certain localities. In the new system, if the average market price falls below a predetermined target price, farmers receive direct payments covering the difference. After a series of pilots, the system has been scaled up nationwide for selected products. The level of "target prices" reflects domestic planting costs to protect farmers from fluctuations in international prices and hence terms of trade. Domestic target prices were above international prices in 2014–16 but have fallen below international levels during the pandemic-induced increase in global food prices in 2020.

10. Lin and Ren (2002) estimate that for the lowest income group they accounted for close to 20 percent of household incomes in 1999.

11. The so-called Grain for Green program targeted the poorest areas—mountainous terrain with steep slopes—and provided farmers in these low-productivity areas with additional income: each farmer received 1,500–2,250 kilograms of grain per hectare per year for reforestation, and 300 yuan per year per hectare in cash payments. The program focused on the upper Yangtze and Yellow Rivers and converted 15 million hectares of cropland, although there have been concerns about sustainability (Heilig et al. 2005; Uchida, Xu, and Rozelle 2004).

12. Estimates suggest that from 1980 to 2001, adoption of improved technology accounted for a quarter of the increase in grain output. Mechanization enhanced the productivity-increasing effect of chemical fertilizers, increasing the fertilizer utilization rate by 15 percent to 20 percent and grain yields by 30–40 kilograms per mu (Xue 2002).

13. Chinese scientist Yuan Longping and his team developed higher-yield rice varieties. Worldwide, a fifth of all rice now comes from species created by hybrid rice following Yuan's breakthrough discoveries, according to the website of the World Food Prize, which he won in 2004.

14. Based on CIKD (forthcoming), chapter 3, and Merotto and Jiang (2021).

15. Based on National Bureau of Statistics (NBS) Yearbook data.

16. In 1991, the labor cost in China was only US$0.20/hour, lower than the costs in its peer countries, such as Indonesia (US$0.40/hour), India (US$0.50/hour), the Philippines (US$0.60/hour), Thailand (US$1.10/hour), and Turkey (US$1.20/hour) (Li and Li 2018).

17. As discussed in the next section, the managed process of labor migration, while potentially positive during the early period of industrialization, has also contributed to rising inequality between households with urban and rural registration, inequalities that were passed on to the next generation because of differences in access to and quality of services and because of the lack of parental support experienced by cohorts of "left-behind children." The authorities have increasingly liberalized the *hukou* system in recent years. Since 2021, hukou registration has been fully freed in cities with fewer than 3 million urban residents, accounting for more than 90 percent of China's cities.

18. There were also many cases of TVEs being established by the new independent entrepreneurs using their savings and borrowing initial capital from family members and relatives, as CIKD field work in Wenzhou has shown.

19. During the first decade of reform, China experienced some setbacks in expanding secondary education, as the opportunity costs of schooling increased with the expansion of earning opportunities for girls and boys (World Bank 1997). However, during the 1990s, secondary education expanded massively, almost doubling enrollment in junior and senior secondary schools by 2000 (National Bureau of Statistics of China 2010, 2020).

20. The progress that China made in reducing stunting, anemia, and endemic infectious diseases is documented in World Bank and World Health Organization (2019).

21. At this stage, China's comparative advantage in cheap labor faded. In 2004, China's average monthly remuneration of manufacturing labor was US$1,800, higher than the figures for India (US$1,600) and Indonesia (US$1,200) (Li and Li 2018). To maintain its competitiveness, China had to move to more capital- and technology-intensive products, further boosting productivity and increasing remuneration.

22. The "Lewis tipping point" or "Lewis turning point" refers to the time in which surplus labor in one sector (typically rural, agriculture) is completely absorbed by another sector (typically, urban, manufacture). It is named after Arthur Lewis, who first described the process of economic transformation (Lewis 1954).

23. Section based on Giles and Mu (2022) and CIKD (forthcoming), chapter 4.

24. For instance, looking at the panel b of figure 3.6, Nigeria saw its share of the urban population quadruple since independence, with only limited gains in per capita incomes. Likewise, Brazil has experienced slow growth since the 1980s, but continued rapid increases in the share of the urban population from about 60 percent to over 85 percent.

25. The 2008 Labor Contract Law and the 2011 Social Security Law opened up access to urban social security and health care programs for migrants, though participation remained low.

26. For instance, in 1985, the Ministry of Public Security established a temporary urban hukou system, which provided a local temporary residence permit to individuals with a legitimate job or business in the city. These guest worker permits (or *zanzhu zheng*) were widely available to migrants starting in 1988 after completing an application to the local public security bureau office. Such a policy effectively guaranteed legal status to migrants, whose presence in cities would otherwise be illegal under the strict hukou regulations.

27. In the 2020 Census the total floating population was 492.8 million, which includes two groups: (1) within-townships floating population (116.9 million), that is, people living in a place within their hukou city but different from their specific location of hukou registration; and (2) between-townships floating population (375.8 million), that is, people living in a place different from their original city (National Bureau of Statistics of China 2021). However, between-townships floating population can also live in rural areas. For that reason, a different data source could help to paint the picture of rural migrant workers in urban areas. This is the National monitoring survey report for rural migrant workers (see appendix A). The 2020 report (http://www.stats.gov.cn/tjsj/zxfb/202104/t20210430_1816933 .html) estimates that the total number of rural migrant workers (with rural hukou but working in nonagricultural sectors for more than six months) reached 285.6 million in 2020, out of which 131.0 million were living in urban areas, which accounted for 14.5 percent of the urban population by residence (902.0 million). Among these rural migrant workers in urban areas, 58.4 percent were within-province rural migrant workers, a figure broadly consistent with the Census.

28. "National Monitoring and Survey Report on Rural Migrant Workers 2018," released by the National Bureau of Statistics.

29. Gains were particularly large for migration to large cities. According to the NBS's Annual Report of Monitoring Survey on National Rural-Urban Migrant Workers (NBS, 2010–2014), in 2008 migrant monthly wages in eastern provinces were 6 percent higher than in other regions; that ratio narrowed by 2013.

30. Using the subsample of the urban population census, Cai and Du (2011) show that in 2005 migrant workers, on average, earned only half the wages of urban residents. Using data from the China Urban Labor Survey, Giles and Park (2014) find that the wage gap for migrants increased from 2001 to 2004 (from 24 percent to 42 percent), but declined to 13 percent by 2010, and disappeared once differences in job characteristics are accounted for (World Bank and DRC 2014). Other sources of

data (NBS; Lu 2012) also point toward a widening of the gap between urban residents' and migrants' wages from 2001 to 2007, which subsequently narrowed again.

31. Analysis done using an urban subsample covering eight provinces of the Integrated Household Survey for 2015, focusing on 1,962 migrant households with all household members living in urban areas. The poverty thresholds used were an absolute poverty line of US$3.1 per day (2011 purchasing power parity) and a relative poverty line defined as 50 percent of the median disposable income per capita of urban residents (14,564.5 yuan/year).

32. The problems associated with urbanization, as discussed in existing literature internationally, include congestion (Abou-Korin 2011), crime (Burton 2000; Jalil and Iqbal 2010; Shopeju 2007), education (Davis 2020; Kayaoglu and Naval 2017), housing (Ooi and Phua 2007; Rahman 1985), transport (Barter 2000), employment (Zhang 2016), health (Godfrey and Julien 2005; Gong et al. 2012; Sclar, Garau, and Carolini 2005), water and sanitation (Costa, Burlando, and Priadi 2016; Van der Bruggen, Borghgraef, and Vinckier 2010), and environmental quality (Imam and Banerjee 2016; Nyambod 2010; Ooi 2009).

33. Under the 2008 Labor Contract Law, all workers, regardless of hukou status, were entitled to participate in urban social insurance programs. But other social services access remained restricted for migrants.

34. For more information on the Rural-Urban Migration in China survey, see appendix A.

35. About 81 percent of them were enrolled in the New Rural Collective Medical System program.

36. With respect to nutritional status of left-behind children, parental migration may not be detrimental and may even be beneficial because young children have lower risk of stunting, being underweight, and wasting (Shi et al. 2020). Chen et al. (2014) and Bai et al. (2018) find that parental migration may have positive impacts on the academic outcomes of the left-behind children. In addition, Zhou et al. (2015) show that for health, nutrition, and education, left-behind children performed as well as or better than children living with both parents.

37. A meta-analysis of 39 academic articles in both English and Chinese confirms the prevalence of depressive symptoms in left-behind children (Wang et al. 2019). Left-behind children are also more likely to engage in unhealthy behaviors, such as smoking and drinking (Yang et al. 2016). In addition, migratory timing and duration affect the probability and timing of children's enrollment in school (Yang and Bansak 2020). Focusing on high school enrollment, Hu (2012) finds that remittances may only partially compensate for the negative impact of an absent parent, and the net negative migration effect on high school enrollment is particularly salient for girls and children from poor households.

38. See Giles and Mu (2022) for a full review of the literature on this topic.

39. Yi, Liu, and Xu (2019) identify a positive impact on the health status of left-behind elderly, whereas Song (2017), Li et al. (2020), and Huang, Lian, and Li (2016) find a negative impact on the physical health of the elderly.

40. The section on inclusive infrastructure development draws on CIKD (forthcoming), chapter 5.

41. For example, Fan and Chan-Kang (2005) report that in 1980 there were only 97 kilometers of roads per thousand square kilometers of land in China, compared with 230 kilometers of roads per thousand square kilometers of land in India and even higher densities in Southeast Asian countries. Benziger (1993) estimates higher density in China, but still below that in India.

42. For a review of this literature, see Rozenberg and Fay (2019).

43. A number of policy documents since the early transition period outline China's approach to user tariffs emphasizing access and affordability, including, for example, the 1983 Directive "Roads and waterways are for all to use," issued by the Ministry of Transport, and the 1988 Water Law. For a comparative review of China's infrastructure policies, see World Bank Benchmarking Infrastructure Annual Reports at https://bpp.worldbank.org/.

44. In 2020, the total length of expressways reached 161,000 kilometers.

45. Looking at China's transport infrastructure, Fan and Chan-Kang (2005) document that the contribution of rural roads to agricultural GDP growth was four times greater than that of major expressways (low-quality rural roads generated 1.57 yuan of agricultural GDP for every yuan as opposed to 0.4 yuan for high-quality roads). Nonagricultural GDP grew by 5 yuan for each yuan spent on rural roads. Fan, Zhang, and Zhang (2004) provide a modeling approach including investments in all types of infrastructure (roads, irrigation, electricity, telecommunications) and estimate that roads had larger effects on agricultural GDP (2.1 yuan for each yuan invested) than electricity (0.54), irrigation (1.8), or telecommunications (1.9). Nonfarm GDP in rural areas was particularly elastic in response to roads (6.7 yuan per yuan invested) and telecommunications (5.1).

46. The Policy Research Office of the All-China Federation of Trade Unions (1998, 318–24).
47. In the period 1980–90, 20 percent of funds directed to underdeveloped regions went to rural infrastructure. The share remained roughly the same in the Seven-Year Priority Poverty Alleviation Program (1994–2000) and the subsequent Outline for Development-Oriented Poverty Reduction for China's Rural Areas (2001–2010). From 2010 to 2019, China's Anti-Poverty Fund allocated more than 33 percent of the total budget to rural infrastructure construction.

References

Abou-Korin, A. A. 2011. "Impacts of Rapid Urbanisation in the Arab World: The Case of Dammam Metropolitan Area, Saudi Arabia." In 5th International Conference and Workshop on Built Environment in Developing Countries, Pulau Pinang, Malaysia, December 6–7.

All-China Federation of Trade Unions. 1998. *The Chinese Trade Unions Statistics Yearbook, 1998*. Beijing: China Statistics Press.

Anderson, Kym, and Will Martin. 2008. "Distortions to Agricultural Incentives in China and Southeast Asia." Agricultural Distortions Working Paper 69, Washington, DC, World Bank.

Bai, Y., L. Zhang, C. Liu, Y. Shi, D. Mo, and S. Rozelle. 2018. "Effect of Parental Migration on the Academic Performance of Left Behind Children in North Western China." *Journal of Development Studies* 54: 1154–70.

Bardhan, Pranab. 2012. *Awakening Giants, Feet of Clay: Assessing the Economic Rise of China and India*. Princeton, NJ: Princeton University Press.

Barter, P. A. 2000. "Urban Transport in Asia: Problems and Prospects for High-Density Cities." *Asia-Pacific Development Monitor* 2 (1): 33–66.

Benziger, Vincent. 1993. "China's Rural Road System during the Reform Period." *China Economic Review* 4 (1): 1–17.

Bikales, B. 2021. "Reflections on Poverty Reduction in China." Swiss Agency for Development and Cooperation, Bern.

Burton, A. 2000. "Wahuni, the Undesirables: African Urbanisation, Crime and Colonial Order in Dar es Salaam, 1919–1961." Doctoral dissertation, SOAS University of London.

Cai, Fang. 2017. "Reform Effects in China: A Perspective of Labor Reallocation." *Economic Research Journal* 7: 4–17.

Cai, Fang, and Yang Du. 2011. "Wage Increases, Wage Convergence, and the Lewis Turning Point in China." *China Economic Review* 22 (4): 601–10.

Cai, Fang, Dewen Wang, and Yang Du. 2002. "Regional Disparity and Economic Growth in China: The Impact of Labor Market Distortions." *China Economic Review* 13 (2–3): 197–212.

Chatterjee, S. 2005. "Poverty Reduction Strategies—Lessons from the Asian and Pacific Region on Inclusive Development." *Asian Development Review* 22: 12–44.

Chen, A., and N. E. Coulson. 2002. "Determinants of Urban Migration: Evidence from Chinese Cities." *Urban Studies* 39 (12): 2189–97.

Chen, Shaohua, and Martin Ravallion. 2004. "Household Welfare Impacts of China's Accession to the World Trade Organization." In *China and the WTO: Accession, Policy Reform and Poverty Reduction Strategies*, edited by D. Bhattasali, S. Li, and W. Martin, 261–82. New York: Oxford University Press.

Chen, Shaohua, and Martin Ravallion. 2021. "Reconciling the Conflicting Narratives on Poverty in China." *Journal of Development Economics* 153 (November).

Chen, X., Q. Huang, S. Rozelle, Y. Shi, and L. Zhang. 2014. "Effect of Migration on Children's Educational Performance in Rural China." In *China's Economic Development*, edited by J. C. Brada, P. Wachtel, and D. T. Yang, 206–24. London: Palgrave Macmillan.

CIKD (Center for International Knowledge on Development). Forthcoming. *Economic Development and Poverty Alleviation in China*. Beijing: CIKD.

Costa, D., P. Burlando, and C. Priadi. 2016. "The Importance of Integrated Solutions to Flooding and Water Quality Problems in the Tropical Megacity of Jakarta." *Sustainable Cities and Society* 20: 199–209.

Davis, J. 2020. "Education and Global Urbanisation." *Urban Schools: Designing for High Density*, edited by H. Taylor and S. Wright, 10–19. London: RIBA Publishing.

de Brauw, Alan, and John Giles. 2018. "Migrant Labor Markets and the Welfare of Rural Households in the Developing World: Evidence from China." *World Bank Economics Review* 32 (1): 1–18.

de Brauw, A., J. Huang, and S. Rozelle. 2004. "The Sequencing of Reform Policies in China's Agricultural Transition." *The Economics of Transition* 12 (3): 427–65.

Deininger, Klaus, and Lyn Squire. 1998. "New Ways of Looking at Old Issues: Inequality and Growth." *Journal of Development Economics* 57 (2): 259–87.

Du, Y., A. Park, and S. Wang. 2005. "Migration and Rural Poverty in China." *Journal of Comparative Economics* 33 (4): 688–709.

Fan, Shenggen. 1991. "Effects of Technological Change and Institutional Reform on Production Growth in Chinese Agriculture." *American Journal of Agricultural Economics* 73 (2): 266–75.

Fan, Shenggen, and Connie Chan-Kang. 2005. "Road Development, Economic Growth, and Poverty Reduction in China." Research Report 138, International Food Policy Research Institute, Washington, DC.

Fan, Shenggen, Linxiu Zhang, and Xiaobo Zhang. 2004. "Reforms, Investment, and Poverty in Rural China." *Economic Development and Cultural Change* 52 (2): 395–421.

Gan, Shiming. 2003. *Statistics of Chinese Township and Village Enterprises (1978–2002)*. Beijing: China Agriculture Press.

Gibson, John. 2020. "Aggregate and Distributional Impacts of China's Household Responsibility System." *Australian Journal of Agricultural and Resource Economics* 64 (1): 14–29.

Giles, John, X. Meng, S. Xue, and G. Zhao. 2021. "Can Information Influence the Social Insurance Participation Decision of China's Rural Migrants?" *Journal of Development Economics* 150: 102645.

Giles, John, and Ren Mu. 2022. "Migration, Growth and Poverty Reduction in China's Villages: A Retrospective and Discussion of Future Challenges." In *Four Decades of Poverty Reduction in China: Background Papers*. Washington, DC: World Bank.

Giles, John, and I. Murtazashvili. 2013. "A Control Function Approach to Estimating Dynamic Probit Models with Endogenous Regressors." *Journal of Econometric Methods* 2 (1): 69–87.

Giles, John, and Albert Park. 2014. "Labor Mobility in China and Implications for an Inclusive Labor Market." Background paper for *Urban China* report, Beijing.

Godfrey, Richard, and Marlene Julien. 2005. "Urbanisation and Health." *Clinical Medicine* 5 (2): 137–41.

Gollin, Douglas, Remi Jedwab, and Dietrich Vollrath. 2016. "Urbanization with and without Industrialization." *Journal of Economic Growth* 21 (1): 35–70.

Gong, P., S. Liang, E. J. Carlton, Q. Jiang, J. Wu, L. Wang, and J. V. Remais. 2012. "Urbanisation and Health in China." *The Lancet* 379 (9818): 843–52.

Guang, Y., Z. Feng, G. Yang, Y. Yang, L. Wang, Q. Dai, C. Hu, K. Liu, R. Zhang, F. Xia, and M. Zhao. 2017. "Depressive Symptoms and Negative Life Events: What Psycho-Social Factors Protect or Harm Left-Behind Children in China?" *BMC Psychiatry* 17: 402.

Guo, Junping, Qingxiang Tan, and Song Qu. 2018. "The Poverty of Rural Migrant Families: An Analytical Framework from the Perspectives of Income, Consumption and Multi-dimensions." *China Rural Economy* (9): 1–16.

Hajj, Hatim, and Setty Pendakur. 2000. "Roads Improvement for Poverty Alleviation in China." East Asia Region Transport Sector Working Paper 1, World Bank, Washington, DC.

Hamnett, C. 2020. "Is Chinese Urbanisation Unique?" *Urban Studies* 57 (3): 690–700.

Harrell, S., W. Yuesheng, H. Hua, G. D. Santos, and Z. Yingying. 2011. "Fertility Decline in Rural China: A Comparative Analysis." *Journal of Family History* 36 (1): 15–36.

Heilig, G., Z. Ming, L. Huaolou, L. Xiubin, and W. Xiuqin. 2005. "Poverty Alleviation in China: A Lesson for the Developing World?" Paper presented at the International Conference on the West Development, August 2–4, Urumqi, China.

Hell, Natalie, and Scott Rozelle. 2020. *Invisible China: How the Urban-Rural Divide Threatens China's Rise*. Chicago: University of Chicago Press.

Herd, Richard. 2020. "Estimating Capital Formation and Capital Stock by Economic Sector in China: The Implications for Productivity Growth." Policy Research Working Paper 9317, World Bank, Washington, DC.

Hertel, Thomas, Fan Zhai, and Zhi Wang. 2004. "Implications of WTO Accession for Poverty in China." In *China and the WTO: Accession, Policy Reform and Poverty Reduction Strategies*, edited by D. Bhattasali, S. Li, and W. Martin, 283–303. New York: Oxford University Press.

Hu, F. 2012. "Migration, Remittances, and Children's High School Attendance: The Case of Rural China." *International Journal of Educational Development* 32: 401–11.

Huang, Philip. 1985. *The Peasant Economy and Social Change in North China*. Stanford, CA: Stanford University Press.

Huang, B., Y. Lian, and W. Li. 2016. "How Far Is Chinese Left-Behind Parents' Health Left Behind?" *China Economic Review*, Special Issue on Human Capital, Labor Markets, and Migration 37: 15–26.

Huang, Jikun, and Scott Rozelle. 1996. "Technological Change: The Re-Discovery of the Engine of Productivity Growth in China's Rice Economy." *Journal of Development Economics* 49 (2): 337–69.

Huang, Jikun, and Scott Rozelle. 2018. "China's 40 Years of Agricultural Development and Reform." In *China's 40 Years of Reform and Development: 1978–2018*, edited by R. Garnaut, L. Song, and C. Cai, 487–507. Acton ACT, Australia: ANU Press.

Huang, Yukon. 2017. *Cracking the China Conundrum: Why Conventional Economic Wisdom Is Wrong*. New York: Oxford University Press.

Imam, A. U., and U. K. Banerjee. 2016. "Urbanisation and Greening of Indian Cities: Problems, Practices, and Policies." *Ambio* 45 (4): 442–57.

Jacoby, H. G. 2002. "Access to Markets and the Benefits of Rural Roads." *Economic Journal* 110 (465): 713–37.

Jalil, H. H., and M. M. Iqbal. 2010. "Urbanisation and Crime: A Case Study of Pakistan." *Pakistan Development Review* 49 (4): 741–55.

Jin, Songqing, Jikun Huang, and Scott Rozelle. 2002. "The Creation and Spread of Technology and Total Factor Productivity in China's Agriculture." *American Journal of Agricultural Economics* 84 (4): 916–30.

Kanbur, Ravi, Yue Wang, and Xiaobo Zhang. 2021. "The Great Chinese Inequality Turnaround." *Journal of Comparative Economics* 49 (2): 467–82.

Kayaoglu, A., and J. Naval. 2017. "Urbanisation, Education and the Growth Backlog of Africa." *Journal of African Economies* 26 (5): 584–606.

Kinnan, C., S.-Y. Wang, and Y. Wang. 2018. "Access to Migration for Rural Households." *American Economic Journal: Applied Economics* 10 (4): 79–119.

Lavely, W., and R. Freedman. 1990. "The Origins of the Chinese Fertility Decline." *Demography* 27 (3): 357–67.

Lewis, W. Arthur. 1954. "Economic Development with Unlimited Supplies of Labor." *The Manchester School* 22 (2): 139–91.

Li, Shi, and Chunbing Xing. 2017. "China's Key Labor Market Trends, Challenges and Policy Implications: Employment, Wage Structure and Labor Productivity." Background paper for World Bank Programmatic Advisory Services and Analytics on Social Protection and Jobs.

Li, Tianxiang, Beibei Wu, Fujin Yi, Bin Wang, and Tomas Baležentis. 2020. "What Happens to the Health of Elderly Parents When Adult Child Migration Splits Households? Evidence from Rural China." *International Journal of Environmental Research and Public Health* 17 (5): 1609.

Li, Xiaohua, and Wenxuan Li. 2018. "The Changing Comparative Advantages of China's Manufacturing in the Four Decades of Reform and Opening-Up." *Southeast Academic Research* 5: 92–103.

Lin, Justin. 1992. "Rural Reforms and Agricultural Growth in China." *American Economic Review* 82 (1): 34–51.

Lin, Justin, Cai Cai, and Zhou Li. 2003. *The China Miracle: Development Strategy and Economic Reform*. Hong Kong SAR, China: Published for the Hong Kong Centre for Economic Research and the International Center for Economic Growth by the Chinese University Press.

Lin, Yifu, and Tao Ren. 2002. "Issue of Chinese Farmers' Tax Burden." China Center for Economic Research, Peking University, 2002.6.

Long, Cheryl, and Xiaobo Zhang. 2011. "Cluster-Based Industrialization in China: Financing and Performance." *Journal of International Economics* 84 (1): 112–23.

Lu, Feng. 2012. "Wage Trends among Chinese Migrant Workers: 1979–2010." *Social Sciences in China* 7: 47–67.

Lugo, Maria Ana, Chiyu Niu, and Ruslan Yemtsov. 2021. "China's Poverty Reduction and Economic Transformation: A Decomposition Approach." Policy Research Working Paper 9849, World Bank, Washington, DC.

Luo, Xubei, and Chiyu Niu. 2019. "E-Commerce Participation and Household Income Growth in Taobao Villages." Policy Research Working Paper 8811, World Bank, Washington, DC.

Merotto, Dino, and Hanchen Jiang. 2021. "What Was the Impact of Creating Better Jobs for More People in China's Economic Transformation? What We Know and Questions for Further Investigation." Jobs Working Paper 62, World Bank, Washington, DC.

Molnar, Margit, Thomas Chalaux, and Qiang Ren. 2017. "Urbanisation and Household Consumption in China." OECD Economics Department Working Paper 1434, OECD Publishing, Paris.

Montalvo, Jose G., and Martin Ravallion. 2010. "The Pattern of Growth and Poverty Reduction in China." *Journal of Comparative Economics* 38 (1): 2–16.

National Bureau of Statistics of China. 2001. *Statistical Yearbook 2001.* Beijing: China Statistical Press.

National Bureau of Statistics of China. 2002. *Statistical Yearbook 2002.* Beijing: China Statistical Press.

National Bureau of Statistics of China. 2010. *Statistical Yearbook 2010.* Beijing: China Statistical Press.

National Bureau of Statistics of China. 2020. *Statistical Yearbook 2020.* Beijing: China Statistical Press.

National Bureau of Statistics of China. 2021. *Statistical Yearbook 2021.* Beijing: China Statistical Press.

Naughton, Barry. 2007. *The Chinese Economy: Transitions and Growth.* Cambridge, MA: MIT Press.

Naughton, Barry. 2018. *The Chinese Economy: Adaptation and Growth.* Second edition. Cambridge, MA: MIT Press.

Nehru, Vikram, Aart Kraay, and Xiaoqing Yu. 1997. *China 2020: Development Challenges in the New Century.* Washington, DC: World Bank Group.

Nyambod, E. M. 2010. "Environmental Consequences of Rapid Urbanisation: Bamenda City, Cameroon." *Journal of Environmental Protection* 1 (1): 15–23.

OECD (Organisation for Economic Co-operation and Development). 2018. "Innovation, Agricultural Productivity and Sustainability in China. Working Party on Agricultural Policies and Markets." Trade and Agricultural Directorate Committee for Agriculture, OECD, Paris.

Ooi, G. L. 2009. "Challenges of Sustainability for Asian Urbanisation." *Current Opinion in Environmental Sustainability* 1 (2): 187–91.

Ooi, G. L., and K. H. Phua. 2007. "Urbanization and Slum Formation." *Journal of Urban Health* 84 (1): 27–34.

Qi, Di, and Yichao Wu. 2016. "Child Income Poverty Levels and Trends in Urban China from 1989 to 2011." *Child Indicators Research* 9: 1043–58.

Rahman, H. 1985. "Urbanisation and the Problem of Slums in Bangladesh." *Community Development Journal* 20 (1): 52–57.

Ravallion, Martin. 2009. "Are There Lessons for Africa from China's Success against Poverty?" *World Development* 37 (2): 303–31.

Ravallion, Martin. 2021. "Poverty in China since 1950: A Counterfactual Perspective." NBER Working Paper 28370, National Bureau of Economic Research, Cambridge, MA.

Ravallion, Martin, and Shaohua Chen. 2007. "China's (Uneven) Progress against Poverty." *Journal of Development Economics* 82: 1–42.

Ravallion, Martin, Shaohua Chen, and Prem Sangraula. 2007. "New Evidence on the Urbanization of Global Poverty." *Population and Development Review* 33 (4): 667–701.

Rodrik, Dani. 2016. "Premature Deindustrialization." *Journal of Economic Growth* 21 (1): 1–33.

Rozenberg, Julie, and Marianne Fay. 2019. *Beyond the Gap: How Countries Can Afford the Infrastructure They Need while Protecting the Planet.* Washington, DC: World Bank.

Sachs, Jeffrey, and Wing They Woo. 1994. "Structural Factors in the Economic Reforms of China, Eastern Europe, and the Former Soviet Union." *Economic Policy* 9 (18): 101–45.

Sclar, E. D., P. Garau, and G. Carolini. 2005. "The 21st Century Health Challenge of Slums and Cities." *The Lancet* 365 (9462): 901–3.

Shi, H., J. Zhang, Y. Du, C. Zhao, X. Huang, and X. Wang. 2020. "The Association between Parental Migration and Early Childhood Nutrition of Left-Behind Children in Rural China." *BMC Public Health* 20: 246.

Shopeju, O. J. 2007. "Urbanisation and Crime in Nigeria." *ASSET: An International Journal* (Series C) 2 (1): 154–63.

Sicular, Terry, and Yaohui Zhao. 2004. "Earnings and Labor Mobility in Rural China: Implications for China's Accession to the WTO." In *China and the WTO: Accession, Policy Reform and Poverty Reduction Strategies,* edited by D. Bhattasali, S. Li, and W. Martin, 239–60. New York: Oxford University Press.

Song, Hongyuan. 2018. *Evolution of China's Agricultural and Rural Economic Policies since Reform and Opening-Up.* China Economic Publishing House (in Chinese), quoted in OECD (2018).

Song, Q. 2017. "Aging and Separation from Children: The Health Implications of Adult Migration for Elderly Parents in Rural China." *Demographic Research* 37: 1761–92.

Straub, Stephane. 2008. "Infrastructure and Growth in Developing Countries: Recent Advances and Research Challenges." Policy Research Working Paper 4460, World Bank, Washington, DC.

Tang, Wanjie, Gang Wang, Tao Hu, Qian Dai, Jiajun Xu, Yanchun Yang, and Jiuping Xu. 2018. "Mental Health and Psychosocial Problems among Chinese Left-Behind Children: A Cross-Sectional Comparative Study." *Journal of Affective Disorders* 241: 133–41.

Uchida, Emi, Jintao Xu, and Scott Rozelle. 2004. "Grain for Green: Cost Effectiveness and Sustainability of China's Conservation Set-Aside Program." Department of Agricultural and Resource Economics, University of California and Center for Chinese Agriculture Policy, CAS.

UNDP (United Nations Development Programme), China Institute for Development Planning at Tsinghua University, and State Information Center. 2019. *China National Human Development Report Special Edition—In Pursuit of a More Sustainable Future for All: China's Historic Transformation over Four Decades of Human Development.* Beijing: China Publishing Group Corporation, China Translation & Publishing House.

UNDP and OPHI (United Nations Development Programme and Oxford Poverty and Human Development Initiative). 2020. *Global Multidimensional Poverty Index 2020. Charting Pathways out of Multidimensional Poverty: Achieving the SDGs.* New York and Oxford: UNDP and OPHI.

Van der Bruggen, B., K. Borghgraef, and C. Vinckier. 2010. "Causes of Water Supply Problems in Urbanised Regions in Developing Countries." *Water Resources Management* 24 (9): 1885–902.

Wang, Y.-Y., L. Xiao, W.-W. Rao, J.-X. Chai, S.-F. Zhang, C. H. Ng, G. S. Ungvari, H. Zhu, and Y.-T. Xiang. 2019. "The Prevalence of Depressive Symptoms in 'Left-Behind Children' in China: A Meta-Analysis of Comparative Studies and Epidemiological Surveys." *Journal of Affective Disorders* 244: 209–16.

World Bank. 1997. *China 2020: Development Challenges in the New Century,* edited by Vikram Nehru, Aart Kraay, and Xiaoqing Yu. Washington, DC: World Bank.

World Bank. 2020. *Infrastructure in Asia and the Pacific: Road Transport, Electricity, and Water and Sanitation Services in East Asia, South Asia, and the Pacific Islands.* Washington, DC: World Bank.

World Bank. 2021. *Eco-compensation in China's Evolving Environmental Management Regime: Status and Trends, and Prospects for River Basin Management.* Washington, DC: World Bank.

World Bank. Forthcoming. *Four Decades of Poverty Reduction in China: Background Papers.* Washington, DC: World Bank.

World Bank and DRC (Development Research Center of the State Council). 2014. *Urban China: Toward Efficient, Inclusive, and Sustainable Urbanization.* Washington, DC: World Bank.

World Bank and DRC (Development Research Center of the State Council). 2019. *Innovative China: New Drivers of Growth.* Washington, DC: World Bank.

World Bank and World Health Organization. 2019. *Healthy China: Deepening Health Reform in China: Building High-Quality and Value-Based Service Delivery.* Washington, DC: World Bank.

Xue, Zhicheng. 2002. "The Role of Agricultural Mechanization in Increasing Food Production." *Guang Xi Agricultural Mechanization* 3: 10–11.

Yang, G., and C. Bansak. 2020. "Does Wealth Matter? An Assessment of China's Rural-Urban Migration on the Education of Left-Behind Children." *China Economic Review* 59: 101365.

Yang, T., C. Li, C. Zhou, S. Jiang, J. Chu, A. Medina, and S. Rozelle. 2016. "Parental Migration and Smoking Behavior of Left-Behind Children: Evidence from a Survey in Rural Anhui, China." *International Journal for Equity in Health* 15: 127.

Yi, F., C. Liu, and Z. Xu. 2019. "Identifying the Effects of Migration on Parental Health: Evidence from Left-Behind Elders in China." *China Economic Review* 54: 218–36.

Yu, N., M. de Jong, S. Storm, and J. Mi. 2013. "Spatial Spillover Effects of Transport Infrastructure: Evidence from Chinese Regions." *Journal of Transport Geography* 28: 56–66.

Zhang, X. Q. 2016. "The Trends, Promises and Challenges of Urbanisation in the World." *Habitat International* 54: 241–52.

Zhang, Xiaobo, Jin Yang, and Shenglin Wang. 2011. "China Has Reached the Lewis Turning Point." *China Economic Review* 22 (4): 542–54.

Zhou, C., S. Sylvia, L. Zhang, R. Luo, H. Yi, C. Liu, Y. Shi, P. Loyalka, J. Chu, A. Medina, and S. Rozelle. 2015. "China's Left-Behind Children: Impact of Parental Migration on Health, Nutrition, and Educational Outcomes." *Health Affairs* 34: 1964–71.

Zhu, Ling. 1997. "Poverty Alleviation during the Transition in Rural China." UNU-WIDER Working Paper, Helsinki.

Zhu, Ling, and Wei He. 2018. "Forty Years' Rural Poverty Reduction in the Chinese Industrialization and Urbanization." *Studies in Labor Economics* 6 (4): 3–31.

Zhu, Ling, and Zhongyi Jiang. 2004. "The Food-for-Work Policy and Expansion of Rural Employment in Poor Areas in Western China." Employment-Intensive Infrastructure Programmes: Socio-Economic Technical Paper 16, International Labour Office, Geneva.

Zhu, Xiaodong. 2012. "Understanding China's Growth: Past, Present, and Future." *Journal of Economic Perspectives* 26 (4): 103–24.

Zhuo, Xian, and Jin Huang. 2019. "Stabilizing the Manufacturing Employment Is the Key Way towards Stable Employment." Research Report of Development Research Center of the State Council, Beijing.

4

Poverty Alleviation Strategies

Introduction

Government policies targeted specifically to poverty reduction have played an important role in improving the lives of the poor in rural areas.[1] Broad economic reforms were complemented by strategies, policies, and programs directly targeted at poverty alleviation. China's poverty alleviation strategy can be characterized as "development oriented," implying a focus on creating economic opportunities as a means to escape poverty. It evolved from an area-based approach, targeting poor counties and villages as a whole, to a set of interventions targeted at poor households. Social protection policies for poor households ("protection-oriented" policies) were developed as a component of this strategy and are increasingly, albeit not yet fully, integrated with China's general social protection instruments (Wang, Qu, and Jia 2017). This point is addressed again below.

Area-based development-oriented policies and targeted poverty alleviation measures have included special financial support and poverty alleviation funds targeting poor areas and households and strategies for coordinated development and assistance between regions. Protection-oriented policies have included specific programs in social assistance, social insurance, social welfare, and other targeted social policies.[2] However, the distinction between these two types of policies should not be drawn too sharply, given that their objectives coincide and their measures can act in complementary ways. For example, in China, public works (a typical protection-oriented cash or food-for-work safety program) were implemented as part of the area-focused assistance with an emphasis on asset creation (in addition to income transfers). On the other hand, some social assistance interventions link beneficiaries of cash transfers to employment programs (for example, Di Bao beneficiaries able to work are referred to employment programs) and thus de facto operate as development oriented. Over time the prevalence of such integrated targeted programs with a focus on productive inclusion has increased.[3] Starting in 2013, the targeted poverty eradication campaign combined development-oriented approaches with the expansion of protection-oriented policies.

Area-based poverty alleviation strategies

Poverty alleviation strategies in China went through four stages, each with a different focus (Liu et al. 2020): relief-type poverty alleviation (1978–85), development-oriented poverty alleviation (1986–2006), development-oriented poverty alleviation combined with social security system reforms (2007–12), and targeted poverty alleviation (since 2013). The first three stages are considered to be area-based poverty alleviation strategies. The list of localities (counties) targeted by special policy interventions has changed over time, and the design of area-based programs was also adapted. China incrementally refined its targeting instruments, reflecting changes in the underlying drivers of poverty—from nationwide approaches to provide basic relief to broad regionally targeted interventions; followed by more narrowly focused programs for poor areas, counties, and villages; and finally to measures targeting specific poor households directly. At the same time, the coverage of social protection programs was rapidly expanded.

Area-based development-oriented poverty alleviation efforts began with the National Poverty Reduction and Development Programs in the mid-1980s, as a response to lagging economic growth and stagnating incomes in some western and central areas of the country (Freije-Rodriguez, Hofman, and Johnston 2019). In 1986, in the broader policy context of letting some areas and people get rich first, the State Council's Leading Group for Poverty Reduction and Development was established "to provide coherence to a large number of poverty reduction initiatives and, in particular, expedite economic development in poor areas" (World Bank 2009, 79). The Leading Group for Poverty Reduction and Development identified poor counties, primarily based on county-level average rural per capita income. Adding provincially designated areas, the list reached nearly 700 counties (of about 2,100 counties in total in 1985) (World Bank 1992). From then on, the focus on poor counties as the unit for policy intervention became an important feature of China's poverty alleviation efforts.

In 1994, the government introduced the "8–7 Poverty Reduction Plan," aiming to lift the majority of the remaining 80 million poor above the then prevailing national poverty line of 206 RMB in 1985 prices (equivalent to US$0.98 per day in 2011 purchasing power parity) during a seven-year period between 1994 and 2000. A new list with 592 nationally designated poor counties was established (World Bank 2001), with a focus on the mountainous regions of the country. The programs under the 8–7 plan included support for the development of farm activities and off-farm employment opportunities (funded with subsidized loans); infrastructure development in roads, electricity, and safe drinking water using predominantly rural workers (food-for-work); universalization of primary education and basic preventive and curative health care; establishment of a monitoring system to hold local governments accountable for the use of budgetary transfers; and the mobilization of a broad group of government and nongovernment actors in a joint poverty reduction effort (see chapter 5).

The 2001–10 Outline for Rural Poverty Alleviation and Development Program further refined the targeting criteria and expanded the scope of government support. By 2001, the share of the rural poor population living in the poverty-stricken counties had declined from 73 percent in 1994 to 62 percent. Refining the geographical target of poverty reduction programs was necessary. The targeting shifted from counties to villages (about 148,000), including some outside the list of poverty-stricken counties.[4] Collectively, the designated villages covered 76 percent of the country's rural poor. Designated villages could apply for projects to support local production and infrastructure (including food-for-work programs, worker training, and agribusiness development including technology extension services; see chapter 3), but also investments in social infrastructure (schools, clinics, community and recreation centers), with a strong participatory approach.

Several studies have tried to quantify the effect of these programs on targeted areas. For instance, Park, Wang, and Wu (2002) find that the large-scale poverty alleviation program in 1986–92 had a modest positive effect on rural income growth in targeted poor counties, and positive spillovers to neighboring counties with higher incomes, suggesting leaks in targeting. Wang, Li, and Ren (2004) find that the 8–7 plan implemented between 1994 and 2000 allocated more resources to poorer counties, and hence targeting aligned well with needs. In addition, the economic growth rate and household income growth of the designated poor counties were larger than the national average (Wang, Li, and Ren 2004). Meng (2013), using a regression discontinuity design, finds that the 8–7 plan resulted in an increase in rural income of approximately 38 percent for counties that were in the program between 1994 and 2000 relative to other counties. Yet, there is evidence that within poor counties, poor households may have benefited less than better-off households (Wang, Li, and Ren 2004).

Beyond their effectiveness in designated poor areas, coverage of the poor through these geographically targeted programs varied over time. The share of the poor living in poverty-stricken areas in each of the plans declined from about 75 percent in the initial year (73 percent in 1994 for the 8–7 plan, and 76 percent in 2001 for the 2001–10 outline) to 62 percent to 63 percent of the total poor by the end of the programs. To address exclusion errors, new plans (including the 2011 Outline for Development-oriented Poverty Reduction for Rural Areas) refined the list of poverty designated areas, each time going to a lower administrative level (from counties to villages). By the end of the 2000s, there was a clear need to complement area-based efforts with a household- or people-oriented approach (World Bank 2009 and box 4.1).[5] The expansion of social protection policies in rural areas since the mid-2000s (covered in the next subsection) and the emergence of targeted poverty alleviation efforts after 2013 (also covered below) reflected this need.

BOX 4.1   **The evolution of poverty targeting: How China used international expertise**

China effectively used the global knowledge of international organizations to refine its pro-poor policies and improve data on poverty. The World Bank, Asian Development Bank, United Nations Development Programme, and many other international organizations assisted with the refinement of China's methodology to measure and monitor poverty, analyzing its profile and evolution and introducing new concepts of poverty. The World Bank's three poverty assessments (1992, 2001, and 2009) informed the reorientation of the government's strategy from broad geographical targeting to a narrower focus on poor villages and households. The Asian Development Bank contributed to these efforts with its methodological tools (such as the multidimensional poverty index used for the identification of poor villages[a]). A hallmark of the

knowledge partnership between China and the international organizations was the close collaboration with Chinese institutions (China's National Bureau of Statistics, the Development Research Center of the State Council, and the Chinese Academy of Social Sciences), ensuring recommendations were embedded in the ongoing national policy debate. The cooperation went beyond technical assistance on analytical issues into testing the practical applicability of recommendations through piloting of new approaches to poverty reduction in projects, which the government was able to test and evaluate, before scaling them nationwide. Examples of these pilots include the multisectoral integrated rural poverty reduction approach and participatory mechanisms for project implementation.

a. In 2000, China announced a shift in targeting of its poverty reduction strategies from counties to villages. Supporting this effort, in 2001, the Asian Development Bank provided technical assistance to identify poor villages in China and created the Participatory Poverty Assessment. In this assessment, infrastructure such as drinking water conditions for humans and animals, power supply rates, and highway coverage were used as important identification criteria for poor villages (Wang et al. 2007; Tang and Liu 2020).

Social protection policies

Until the middle of the 2000s, the provision of basic social security, access to social services, as well as old-age income protection for rural households was the responsibility of the communes. However, with the deepening of land reforms, changes to rural taxation, and the expansion of market-based economic activities in the countryside, the communes increasingly lost their role as guarantors of basic social protection.[6] Government programs funded with budgetary transfers from higher levels of government took on greater importance. A significant part of this expansion was direct cash transfers to the poor in the form of social assistance to protect those who are left behind in the process of economic development. The major programs expanding social protection to rural areas are listed in table 4.1.

By the mid-2000s, old-age poverty emerged as a new policy concern given the rapid aging of China's rural population, and subsidized universal pension schemes were started as pilots and then expanded nationwide. Between 2009 and 2013, China tripled the number of people covered by the old-age pension system (ILO 2015). The urban and the rural resident pension schemes were unified beginning in 2014. However, the benefit level of the rural resident pension remains below half the value of the rural poverty line (table 4.1). By 2020, almost all of the eligible rural population received a basic pension and universal medical insurance package.[7] This provided basic income security to the rural population.

After a series of pilots, the minimum income guarantee program (Di Bao) for rural areas was launched nationwide in 2007 and expanded rapidly, reaching over 52 million beneficiaries by 2010, but falling in coverage to 34.5 million by 2019. Di Bao was a fundamental change—for the first time the government offered a minimum income guarantee to the eligible population whose income was below the Di Bao line (set at the local level). Di Bao eligibility was checked with the help of a registry of the population using a multidimensional definition of poverty (income, assets, housing condition, education, health, employment). However, local fiscal conditions often dictated that the rural Di Bao income eligibility line was set very low, reducing its coverage of the extreme poor. Thus, in 2015, the Di Bao line was below the rural poverty line in about half of the poor counties (Wang, Qu, and Jia 2017). In subsequent years, in conjunction with the targeted poverty reduction strategy, Di Bao lines in all counties were adjusted to be above the official rural poverty line. In practice, however, eligibility for the scheme remains determined by local rules that de facto exclude most of the able bodied from receipt of the Di Bao, even if their household income falls short of the minimum standard (Golan, Sicular, and Umapathi 2017). Once a household gets accepted in Di Bao, it typically receives multiple other social assistance benefits listed in table 4.1 under social assistance, such as education and medical assistance (Wang, Qu, and Jia 2017).

The effects of some of these programs on poverty reduction have been studied and documented using survey data. For example, Li, Zhan, and Shen (2017), using data from the 2013 Chinese Household Income Project survey, find that public transfers reduced rural poverty by 4 percentage points (from 12.3 percent to 8.4 percent).[8] Within public transfers, contributory pensions and the new (largely noncontributory) rural pension scheme accounted for half of this effect, while the Di Bao social assistance transfers contributed about 0.6 percentage points, and various other subsidies contributed another percentage point. More narrowly focusing on rural Di Bao, Golan, Sicular, and Umapathi (2017) arrive at estimates of similar orders of magnitude. The greater coordination of Di Bao with the targeted poverty reduction campaign has improved the coverage of the rural poor in recent years, but information platforms and administration remain fragmented (Wang, Qu, and Jia 2017; Westmore 2017). Some groups, such as young rural migrant workers and informally employed workers, fall outside the coverage of China's Di Bao system and are also less likely to be covered by other forms of social protection (table 4.1). For instance, in 2017, only 17 percent of migrant workers were covered by an unemployment insurance scheme (World Bank 2020). Low-wage migrants tend to receive no or very little support when they fall below the urban local low-income threshold (Di Bao line)[9] because the urban-rural binary social aid system provides inadequate protection for them.

TABLE 4.1   Main social protection programs in rural and urban China, 2019 or latest available data

Social protection program	Start year[a]	Number of participants or beneficiaries	Annual spending (RMB) [share of GDP]	Coverage (percent of eligible population)	Average benefit level
Social assistance			**805.3 billion [0.8 percent]**		
Urban Di Bao	1997	8.6 million	52 billion [0.05 percent]	1.20	503 RMB/month
Rural Di Bao	2002	34.5 million	112 billion [0.11 percent]	7.90	272 RMB/month
Tekun[b]	1985	4.7 million	38.3 billion [0.04 percent]	1	727 RMB/month
Medical assistance	2003	87.5 million recipients of subsidy; 70.5 million cases for medical assistance	50.2 billion [0.05 percent]	n.a.	1,123 RMB/case for inpatient assistance; 93 RMB/case for outpatient assistance
Disaster relief	1978	60 million	14 billion [0.01 percent]	30	n.a.
Temporary assistance	2014	9.9 million	14 billion [0.01 percent]	n.a.	181 RMB/month
Housing assistance[c]	2009	40 million (5 million of which are rural)	294 billion [0.3 percent]	n.a.	7,350 RMB/year
Education assistance	n.a.	91 million	138 billion [0.14 percent]	n.a.	1,516 RMB/year
Employment assistance	2016	5.4 million (mostly urban)	78 billion [0.08 percent]	63	n.a.
Food-for-work fund	1985	n.a.	41 billion [0.04 percent]	n.a.	n.a.
Social insurance		**1.4 billion**	**7,566 billion [7.6 percent]**		
Urban employee pension scheme	1993	455 million participants (328 million contributors and 127 million beneficiaries)	4,878 billion [4.9 percent]	64 percent of population with urban *hukou* ages 15+	3,302 RMB/month
Resident pension scheme (social pension)	2014 Rural and Urban resident pension schemes merged	542 million participants (381 million contributors and 160 million beneficiaries)	311 billion [0.3 percent]	46 percent of urban and rural population ages 15+ (when combined with Urban employee pension scheme, coverage is 90 percent)	Average 162 RMB/month (minimum 88 RMB/month)
Urban	2011	24 million participants	n.a.	4	n.a.
Rural	2009	517 million participants	n.a.	85	n.a.
Urban employee basic medical insurance	n.a.	329 million participants	1,266 billion [1.3 percent]	74	n.a.
Resident basic medical insurance	2016 merged with Urban resident basic medical insurance	1,025 million	819 billion [0.8 percent]	73	n.a.
Work injury insurance	2008	254 million participants; 2 million beneficiaries (urban)	81.7 billion [0.08 percent]	33	42,090 RMB/case

(table continued next page)

TABLE 4.1 Main social protection programs in rural and urban China, 2019 or latest available data (Continued)

Social protection program	Start year[a]	Number of participants or beneficiaries	Annual spending (RMB) [share of GDP]	Coverage (percent of eligible population)	Average benefit level
Unemployment insurance	1997	205 million participants; 5 million beneficiaries (urban)	133 billion [0.13 percent]	46	n.a.
Maternity insurance	2008	214 million participants (urban)	76 billion [0.07 percent]	55	n.a.

Sources: Freije-Rodriguez and Zhao 2021 and World Bank estimations based on reports by the Ministry of Civil Affairs, the Ministry of Human Resources and Social Security, and the National Healthcare Security Administration.

Note: Rural official poverty line in 2019 was 260 RMB/month. GDP = gross domestic product; n.a. = not applicable; RMB = renminbi.

a. Start year refers to the first pilot implementation. The full nationwide scale-up typically occurred several years after the start; for example, for urban Di Bao the first state council resolution started official pilots of the program, which came to full scale in 2002; rural Di Bao pilots started in 2002 and scaled up nationally to all rural areas in 2007. Unemployment insurance had been operating since 1997, but the current nationwide setup was established in 2008.

b. Tekun (meaning "extreme [poor]") is a program that emerged in 2014 by combining the former Sanwu (literally "three nos"—people with no ability to work, no source of income, or any caregiver providing for them) program in urban areas with Wubao (or "Five Guarantees"—providing clothes, food, medical care, housing, and burial expenses for the destitute) in rural areas. The objective of Tekun is to provide support for basic daily expenses, including care and medical treatment to the "three nos" population. Tekun recipients cannot benefit from other social assistance programs.

c. Includes housing subsidy, nursing home funding, mental hospitals, homes for orphans, and so on.

The expansion of coverage rates by social protection programs has resulted in high coverage by international standards. Using 2013 Chinese Household Income Project data from the ASPIRE portal,[10] the World Bank calculated that as early as 2013 China's coverage rate among the poorest 20 percent of rural households of the social protection system (social assistance and social insurance) was very high, at 76 percent. This is higher than both the average for the East Asia and Pacific region (45 percent) and the average for upper-middle-income countries (57 percent). On the other hand, considering solely cash transfer programs, only 18 percent of the poorest quintile are covered. Most of the beneficiaries in this quintile were getting social assistance through other channels: 54 percent were covered by subsidies (such as for agriculture, education, medical, and housing) and 19 percent by in-kind programs. Recent updated estimates, which consider nonmonetary forms of assistance from other sources, suggest that China has achieved almost complete coverage of the poor by some form of social assistance, although benefit levels often remain inadequate (World Bank 2021).

At the onset of the poverty eradication campaign institutional coordination between social assistance programs and targeted development-oriented poverty alleviation was limited, but recent evidence increasingly points toward relatively good coordination between social assistance and poverty reduction (World Bank 2021). Despite improved monitoring of beneficiaries, fiscal constraints continue to determine coverage rates and benefit levels at the local level. Unfortunately, only a few studies have examined the interaction of development-oriented poverty reduction strategies with targeted social assistance policies to better understand whether the latter are more effective when combined with the former, or whether social transfers create welfare dependency, as feared by some Chinese observers (one exception is Wang, Qu, and Jia [2017]). Such studies would also contribute to the design of poverty reduction policies going forward, taking into account their cost and efficiency.

Targeted poverty alleviation strategy

In the past decade, China's poverty reduction strategy was adjusted once again after the new leadership defined poverty alleviation by 2020 as one of the top priorities. The 2011 Outline for Development-oriented Poverty Reduction for China's Rural Areas and the expanded and refined Targeted Poverty Alleviation strategy since 2013 marked a more decisive shift from area-based to household-centered poverty targeting. In 2011, new areas were added to the list of poverty-stricken counties, which reached a total of 832. By then, the previously designated poor villages accounted for less than two-thirds of the total rural poor in the country and a recalibration was called for.

The targeted poverty alleviation strategy aimed to help all of the remaining poor achieve incomes above the national income poverty line and meet a set of multidimensional goals.[11] The strategy spanned the whole process from poverty identification to poverty exit, determining whom to help, who should help, how to help, how to exit, and how to avoid poverty reoccurrence. The strategy was based on a comprehensive database of targeted households and their specific needs, complemented with local knowledge to find appropriate solutions,[12] and the definition of clear lines of accountability for results. Instruments included policies for economic development and income generation, relocation and resettlement, ecological protection and compensation, education, and social protection.[13] The strategy overall remained focused on creating the conditions for poor households to find employment and a stable source of income to lift themselves out of poverty, while combining this with household-specific support in key areas such as housing, skills development, health care, job search, and where necessary, income transfers.

The identification of poor households integrated top-down and bottom-up approaches. The top-down approach included the National Bureau of Statistics–determined "quotas" of poor households, both nationwide and in each province, according to the 2010 national poverty standard, as a baseline for bottom-up identification. The total remaining rural poor population was estimated to amount to about 100 million people. The quotas were broken down to each administrative level. Under the bottom-up approach, about 800,000 officials were dispatched to carry out "Precise Poverty Identification" (Jingzhun Shibie). On the basis of the quota allocated, each team registered every poor household regardless of whether they resided in poor counties. Notably, household income ceased to be the only criterion for identification. Because local governments often did not have accurate and reliable income records for all rural households, they verified household assets such as housing and durable goods to supplement the income-based poverty line. To include all qualified households, individual provinces were allowed to register up to 10 percent larger populations than their quotas.[14]

The implementation of the strategy was not always smooth. Errors of inclusion (households identified as poor that did not need assistance) and exclusion (poor households that failed to receive adequate support) resulting from governance weaknesses in rural areas emerged early on given the lack of reliable income survey data at the village level. This led to additional verifications and the reidentification of poor households, as well as close supervision of declared "exits" from poverty (State Council 2021). The latter proved particularly important in the context of the significant incentives created for local officials to achieve poverty reduction targets (box 4.2). Local feedback mechanisms were also created to support top-down accountability.[15]

The targeted poverty alleviation strategy was endowed with generous government funding. From 2013 to 2020, the government steadily increased funds to meet the challenge. Allocations from the Anti-Poverty Fund (APF) of the central, provincial, and local governments totaled nearly 1.6 trillion yuan (figure 4.1), including 660.1 billion yuan from the central budget. Since 2016, the allocation of funds to poverty reduction has increased substantially, both at the central and local levels.[16] Recently published estimates for 2020 indicate that central funds for poverty alleviation reached 146.5 billion yuan, and APF resources from subnational governments reached 208.3 billion yuan, together representing about 0.35 percent of gross domestic product (GDP). Nonbudget sources also contributed to poverty alleviation during 2013–20, including more than 710 billion yuan in small loans and 100.5 billion yuan in government and social assistance funds from nine eastern provincial-level administrative units to paired units in poor provinces. Official estimates (State Council 2021) suggest the total amount of assistance provided (including other funds such as loans, financial credits, and assistance from eastern provinces) may have reached up to 1 percent of GDP in 2020, including a variety of other funds, discussed further below.

The resources of the APF are allocated to support several programs set forth by the State Council Leading Group Office of Poverty Alleviation and Development, the National

BOX 4.2   Human resources and incentives for targeted poverty alleviation

China has relied on the personal responsibility of officials at different levels for achieving policy goals. The targeted poverty alleviation strategy has likewise relied on a system of incentives, field assignments, and results indicators (see box 5.1 for a discussion of these instruments). The implementation of the targeted poverty alleviation strategy became the responsibility of Party secretaries at all five administrative levels (the Communist Party of China Central Committee, provincial committee, municipal committee, county-level committee, and village

committee). Leadership at these levels was monitored under a rigorous annual evaluation conducted by upper-level agencies and third-party institutions. Unprecedented human capital inflows from the central and upper-level governments enhanced the human capacity of impoverished villages in a short period. As of early 2020, 255,000 work teams and a total of 2.9 million cadres from governmental agencies above the county level and state-owned enterprises had been deployed to impoverished and vulnerable villages (Xi 2020).

FIGURE 4.1   Central and provincial Anti-Poverty Fund allocations, 2001–20

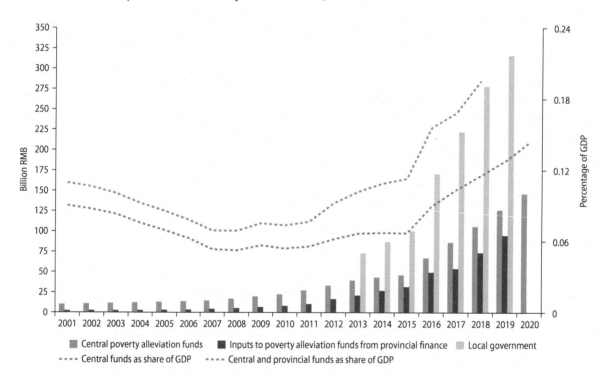

Source: Freije-Rodriguez and Zhao 2021, based on Yearbook of China's Poverty Alleviation and Development 2019.
Note: Some provinces did not disclose specific amounts of their central or provincial Anti-Poverty Fund. GDP = gross domestic product.

Development and Reform Commission, and other ministries.[17] Greater horizontal coordination and synergy emerged among government departments after the adoption of targeted poverty alleviation. In particular, significant authority and budget execution flexibility were given to local governments, as piloted, for instance, in the context of the World Bank–supported Poverty Reduction Program for Results operation in Guangxi, launched in 2016. Unusually for local budget execution, resources associated with targeted poverty alleviation were pooled, allowing county governments flexibility in targeting specific local needs.

In addition, and outside the budget of the APF, functional (sectoral or "industrial") government departments have contributed to improving the standard of living in poor areas (including through financial transfers, centrally funded investments, and the mobilization of human resources), with total funds estimated to be well above the APF budget itself. A particularly important mechanism of support for poverty reduction outside of the resources of the APF has been the twinning of rich and poor provinces and counties, a mechanism that was formed as early as 1996 and has gained in prominence since 2014 (see box 4.3).

Complementing the APF and provincial twinning programs are various financial resources from state-owned banks, commercial banks, and other financial institutions. As of the end of 2020, more than 710 billion yuan of microcredit had been issued, supporting more than 15 million poor households (State Council 2021). All major Chinese state-owned banks are actively involved in supplying poverty alleviation loans, supporting local small and medium enterprises and entrepreneurs interested in investing in poor counties, financing local infrastructure investments, and helping improve the financial literacy of customers from poor households. The policy-based banks, such as the Agricultural Development Bank of China, played an important role in setting up a matchmaking platform for attracting and facilitating investment in poor counties. The Ministry of Finance and other departments set up an online platform, supporting budget units of various government bodies to prioritize the purchase of agricultural products from the 832 poverty-stricken counties.

Other enterprises, individuals, and civil society organizations have been mobilized to support the poverty elimination agenda. Although it is hard to gauge the amount of resources invested in these initiatives, it is believed that they may have grown significantly over recent years to reach an estimated 0.5 percent of GDP (World Bank Group estimate based on State Council 2021). Finally, urban residents have been mobilized to buy products from poverty-stricken counties (Hou 2020).

BOX 4.3 **East-West collaboration from the perspective of a poverty-stricken district in Ningxia Autonomous Region**

Ningxia, a poor province of China, has benefited from East-West Poverty Alleviation Cooperation since 1996. From 1996 to 2016, one poor county in Ningxia was paired with a county in the relatively rich coastal province of Fujian on a two-year rotating basis. In November 2016, the partnership between Yuanzhou District in Ningxia and Mawei District in Fujian was fixed for the duration of the poverty reduction campaign. The cooperation between Yuanzhou and Mawei covers six aspects: funding, public servants, employment, health and education, business and investment, and skills development.

Funding. Each year, the provincial government of Fujian provides dedicated funding to Ningxia. The government of Ningxia transfers the money to each locality based on their conditions and needs.

Additionally, enterprises and twinned districts in Fujian provide funding directly to Yuanzhou. The amounts have increased considerably over time: from 5 million yuan in 2012 to 61.6 million yuan in 2020. These transfers are in addition to the 12.7 million yuan donated by other companies and social organizations. The funding is used for infrastructure construction, subsidies to the impoverished households, vocational training, and other projects.

Public servants. Two officials from Fujian are sent to Yuanzhou for a term of two years, to work as the deputy head and the assistant head of the district, funded by Fujian. Their main responsibilities are to facilitate the cooperation and help the local government in its efforts to reduce poverty.

(box continued next page)

In 2020, six technical experts were also exchanged. Once the officials and technical personnel complete their term, they are likely to receive promotion. Reciprocally, officials from Yuanzhou District are sent to work in Fujian.

Labor cooperation. Workers from Yuanzhou are welcomed to work in factories in Fujian. The local government in Fujian provides a one-time subsidy of 13,500 yuan to each worker, once the person has worked for six consecutive months. The government of Yuanzhou District provides an additional subsidy. Between January and November of 2020, Fujian received 2,972 workers from Yuanzhou, with almost half from registered poor households.

Health care and educational support. Each year, the Fujian government selects a team of doctors and teachers from its public hospitals and schools to work in Yuanzhou District for three to six months. Doctors help treat patients that were previously untreatable by local hospitals. The visiting doctors and teachers are expected to be promoted and to receive professional titles once they return.

Business development and investment. To facilitate business exchanges, the local governments organized a visit by Fujian merchants to Yuanzhou to explore business opportunities. In 2019, Rong Qiao Group, a Fujian real estate company, invested 1 billion yuan to build a large-scale beef processing plant, making it the largest Fujian investment in Yuanzhou. Based on the latest forecast, the plant could generate over 300 job opportunities. The government also helps businesses from Yuanzhou to sell their products, such as beef and lamb, wine, and other agricultural products, in Fujian.

Training. Under the framework of partner assistance, in 2018, the Fujian company SCUD Group built a vocational school in Yuanzhou. The school is free for all eligible local students, with expenses covered by the company, including lodging, food, tuition, and other fees. The government financed part (3.2 million yuan) of the investment from fiscal resources transferred from Fujian, and the rest (8 million yuan) came from SCUD. Students receive three years of training, including a year of internship at the company headquarters in Fuzhou. Graduate students are guaranteed a position at the company's factories, but they are not obliged to work there. As of the end of 2020, the school had recruited 449 students, including 269 from registered poor households. The first batch of graduates, 44 students, are now working in the company as full-time employees, earning an average monthly wage of 4,000 to 5,000 yuan.

Source: Center for International Knowledge on Development background paper on Fujian-Ningxia partnership (World Bank, forthcoming).

Institutional innovations for targeted poverty alleviation were boosted by digital technologies for better efficiency. Digital technologies have facilitated poverty targeting and also contributed to improving the connectivity of poor households to markets through e-commerce and facilitation of access to finance through new digital finance platforms (box 4.4). China's access to and investment in digital connectivity, and the quality of the analog complements, including good transport, energy, and other public infrastructure, as well as significant improvements in human capital, are not easy to replicate in many developing countries (Luo and Niu 2019). But China arguably has found an effective way to harness its digital capabilities for the benefit of targeted poverty reduction.

The combined efforts of the multiple actors involved in the national targeted poverty reduction campaign had by the end of 2020 succeeded in eliminating "extreme poverty." On February 25, 2021, a new national poverty census was completed, and the eradication of absolute poverty was officially declared.

This achievement is matched by considerable improvements in access to public infrastructure services. A total of 1.1 million kilometers of rural roads were built or improved in poor areas. The reliability rate of rural power supply reached 99 percent. The irrigation and drainage facilities in poor areas have been greatly improved, as have flood control and drought relief and mitigation capabilities. More than 98 percent of the poor villages have access to optical fiber and 4G connectivity.[18]

BOX 4.4   How digital technologies were leveraged for targeted poverty alleviation

Poverty targeting

Digital technologies improved the accuracy and effectiveness of poverty alleviation by enhancing targeting, selection of antipoverty measures, implementation of assistance projects, and funds utilization. Guizhou province took the lead in using digital technologies and an integrated data platform for poverty reduction work. The Poverty Alleviation and Development Office of Guizhou put into use the Guizhou Poverty Alleviation Cloud platform, which pooled information from 7.48 million registered poor (as of 2012) and applied geographic information systems to locate the poor at the village level. It provided data updates with personal computer and app terminals instead of paper forms, bringing about data sharing among departments and timely announcement of policies and specific actions, such as matching of employment vacancies to job seekers. More than 409,000 users of the platform include poverty alleviation department officials at each administrative level, persons in charge of local assistance, the first secretary, and the local poverty reduction team.

The platform also records poverty alleviation project types, start and end dates, and the number of beneficiaries, which supports decision-making for industry development, employment, migration and relocation, and other assistance adapted to household conditions. The distribution and payment of various subsidies and livelihood funds to each poor household can also be searched. It presents the specific uses of the central and local Anti-Poverty Fund and integration funds, and comprehensively tracks fund use and investment by beneficiaries. It can also screen out households that do not meet the requirements for poverty registration, and thus help optimize the efficiency of poverty alleviation resources use.

*Inclusive business models of
e-commerce platforms*

E-commerce platforms have greatly lowered the threshold for small and micro businesses to enter large markets. The division of labor brought by the e-commerce industry created employment opportunities for the poor in various fields, including processing, logistics, packaging, and customer service. More than 5 percent of total employment in China is in e-commerce. E-commerce platform companies such as Alibaba and JD.com have proactively developed inclusive business models and incorporated philanthropic programs to enhance market access, income growth, and capacity building in poverty-stricken areas (World Bank and Alibaba Group 2019). In 2019, online retail sales in 832 poverty-stricken counties reached 239.2 billion yuan (MOFCOM 2020[a]). The National Rural E-commerce Comprehensive Demonstration Project has contributed to the income growth of nearly 3 million registered impoverished households (NDRC 2018[b]). By 2020, turnover of products from national-level poverty-stricken counties reached more than 200 billion yuan on the Alibaba platform (Alibaba Group 2020). Online retailing has created over 28 million jobs in rural China (CIECC 2018[c]). In addition, rural e-commerce also benefits the most vulnerable groups such as women and the elderly. From April 2015 to March 2017, 1.12 million people from 765 national-level poverty-stricken counties took 559 online courses offered by Alibaba, which can be accessed from about 92 percent of these counties (Alibaba Group 2017[d]).

Digital inclusive finance

The digital financial institutions established by internet companies make use of transaction data from e-commerce platforms to accurately analyze the transaction behaviors of poor households or micro businesses and portray their credit ratings. The poor population and micro businesses in rural areas could have access to financial services such as digital credit, mobile payment, and internet insurance. The application of digital technology to financing helps provide new solutions to the "last mile" problem of inclusive finance, contributing to lessening the impact of insufficient mortgages for the poor. However, the accuracy of digital models in depicting borrower risk profiles should not be overestimated, and the roles of other actors are essential. Relevant regulatory reforms (for example, requiring separate licenses for the personal credit reporting businesses of fintech conglomerates, refining personal data protection law, and others) are underway.

The number of online banking accounts in rural areas totaled 612 million in 2018, covering

(box continued next page)

63.22 percent of the rural population[e]; the number of annual online banking payments topped 10.21 billion; and payment receipt services provided by banks for rural electronic transactions reached 578.34 billion yuan (People's Bank of China 2019[f]). Financial institutions cooperate with internet companies to further expand the financial coverage of rural populations.

Since its establishment in 2015, China's first cloud computing–based commercial bank, MYbank, has provided contactless loans to more than 4 million clients in 146 poverty-stricken counties. In 2017, JD.com launched a digital agricultural loan. Based on a quantitative model of agricultural production and the historical production data of farmers, it grants credit to farmers without collateral. In two years, this project has collaborated with more than 100 cooperatives in Shandong, Hebei, Henan, and others, providing loans of roughly 1 billion yuan, with a zero overdue rate (Jiang and Liu 2020).

a. http://www.mofcom.gov.cn/article/i/jyjl/l/202006/20200602969096.shtml.
b. http://www.gov.cn/xinwen/2018–04/20/content_5284269.htm#2.
c. http://www.xinhuanet.com/2018–06/06/c_1122943923.htm.
d. AliResearch (Alibaba Group). "E-commerce for China's Poverty Reduction: Research Report on E-commerce for Poverty Reduction and Inclusive Development" (电子商务助力中国减贫——电商减贫与普惠发展研究报告). August 30, 2017.
e. Coverage is estimated by dividing the total number of online banking accounts in the rural area (612 million) by the total rural population of 968 million as of the end of 2018. However, one rural resident may own more than one online bank account (from different banks). It also depends on how the rural population is defined (given that there is a "floating" population that is counted as rural if holding rural hukou). A relevant Findex indicator is defined as "Used a mobile phone or the internet to access an account, rural (% age 15+)." China's 2017 data have much lower coverage, at 35 percent.
f. http://www.gov.cn/xinwen/2019–04/02/content_5378936.htm.

Although the targeted poverty reduction campaign has achieved its objectives, the data needed for a robust evaluation of its costs and benefits are currently not available. Given the sheer scale of resource mobilization from budgetary and nonbudgetary sources, the efficiency and sustainability of government efforts since 2013 is of particular interest. A first exploration in this direction is made by Freije-Rodriguez and Zhao (2021). Exploiting provincial-level data from 2010 through 2017, the authors aim to estimate the impact of public expenditure on poverty reduction programs and social assistance. They find that economic growth had less impact on poverty reduction in recent years, whereas antipoverty programs (funded through central and provincial governments' antipoverty funds) had a positive effect. Nevertheless, the effect needs further study: a 10 percent increase in antipoverty funds per rural poor brings a poverty rate of reduction in the 0.16 to 0.77 percent range (Freije-Rodriguez and Zhao 2021, 45).[19]

Unfortunately, Freije-Rodriguez and Zhao are not able to break the effectiveness of government programs down into separate components, which would be of interest to draw more specific lessons for policy. Moreover, the analysis is not able to incorporate data on other government programs, such as subsidized loans or subsidies to education and agricultural inputs, that may be contributing to poverty reduction. By the same token, a large share of the funds mobilized under the government's poverty eradication campaign have remained outside the budget system and are not well documented, further complicating an evaluation of the campaign's efficiency and sustainability.

There is thus scope for more research going forward, to learn lessons from China's success in reaching the goal of absolute poverty eradication. This is all the more important because China has decided to keep the levels of support to households that graduated from poverty in place for another five years to prevent any relapses into poverty. This volume returns to the question of

TABLE 4.2 **Share of registered poor households achieving "three guarantees" and safe drinking water**

		Share of registered poor households (%)	
	"Three guarantees" and safe drinking water	National impoverished counties	Other counties
Compulsory education (% of school-age children in registered poor households)	Attend school	98.83	99.06
	Take education at home	0.26	0.57
	Absence due to physical reasons, suspension, postponement of enrollment, graduation from junior high school, and others	0.91	0.37
Basic medical insurance (% of residents in registered poor households)	Participate in the basic medical insurance program for urban and rural residents	99.85	99.74
	Participate in employee basic medical insurance program	0.14	0.24
	Newborns who are in the process of insurance enrollment, or people in a special state of protection such as joining the army, or other conditions that do not need insurance	0.01	0.01
Safe housing (% of registered poor households)	Current house was assessed as safe, or living in other safe housing	43.74	58.26
	Realize housing safety through dilapidated building renovation policy	42.25	34.70
	Realize housing safety through relocation poverty alleviation project	14.01	7.04
Safe drinking water (% of registered poor households)	Water supply to home	93.67	84.25
	No water supply to home, but it is convenient to get water	6.33	15.75
	No shortage of water	99.86	99.95
	Water supply is basically guaranteed, but there is water shortage for a few days	0.14	0.05

Sources: Communiqué on the National Poverty Alleviation Census (No. 2) published by the National Bureau of Statistics of China and the State Council Leading Group Office of Poverty Alleviation and Development census on February 25, 2021.

the way forward for China's poverty reduction efforts in chapter 6. Before doing so, chapter 5 examines China's poverty reduction in a comparative perspective to draw lessons for other developing countries.

Notes

1. This section is based on CIKD (forthcoming, chapters 6 and 7) and Freije-Rodriguez and Zhao (2021).
2. Those include, but are not limited to, social guarantees, which go beyond the traditional scope of social protection and include targeted programs in health, education, and housing.
3. For global evidence on productive inclusion, see Partnership for Economic Inclusion, https://www.peiglobal.org/.
4. The World Bank's 2001 Poverty Assessment called for refocusing the selection of beneficiaries of poverty reduction programs from counties to villages, which helped shift to the selection of 148,000 poor villages and the introduction of community-centered programs since the early 2000s (World Bank 2001).
5. "From poor areas to poor people" was the theme of the World Bank's 2009 Poverty Assessment, which illustrated that the area-focused poverty strategy (592 poverty-stricken counties) was missing a significant proportion of the rural poor (World Bank 2009).
6. In urban areas, social protection services were provided by state enterprises or other work units. With the reform of state enterprises and the emergence of urban unemployment for the first time, the need arose to develop government social protection policies. The efforts in urban areas preceded the expansion of social protection to rural areas.
7. The introduction of health insurance coverage alleviated some of the spending pressures (with the reimbursement rate for eligible hospitalization expenses of the rural impoverished population reaching 80 percent) and considerably reduced out-of-pocket spending for the poor. Still, some estimates

suggest that the proportion of the poor due to illness in 2018 was about 40 percent (Zhou, Guo, and Liu 2020).

8. Strictly speaking, the authors calculate poverty with and without incomes from public transfers. This means that, in the absence of behavioral response, the elimination of public transfers would increase the poverty rate by 4 percentage points. In that sense, it can be seen as an upper bound.

9. By 2020, in most provinces the minimum wage was twice as high as the Di Bao line. Hence, formal sector migrant workers who benefit from at least the minimum wage would be above the Di Bao line. However, a large proportion of rural migrants work in informal occupations. In addition, they typically support other family members, in which case the wage may not be sufficient to cover the per capita Di Bao standard.

10. ASPIRE = Atlas of Social Protection Indicators of Resilience and Equity (http://datatopics .worldbank.org/aspire/).

11. These are referred to in China as the "two no-worries" and "three guarantees." "Two no-worries" refers to the satisfaction of essential food and clothing needs, represented in monetary terms as household expenditure above the food and nonfood poverty threshold. "Three guarantees" refers to achieving compulsory education and having access to basic medical care and safe housing. Safe drinking water was later added to the list. Each county was given a financial transfer to achieve the three guarantees. For example, the education guarantee includes the monetary value of government assistance to the poor to access preschool, compulsory primary and secondary, and general higher education, such as subsidy for tuitions, fee waivers, boarding cost subsidies, value of school meals provided for free, and various scholarships and education grants. The monetary value of these guarantees differed across poor counties because of the different investment needs required to achieve universal coverage with the basic public services package. As shown in CIKD (forthcoming, chapter 1, "The Process of Poverty Reduction in China"), education, health, housing, and drinking water benefits were valued between 3,000 RMB and slightly more than 8,000 RMB per person per year among three case study counties, Xunwu County in Jiangxi province, Minhe County in Qinghai province, and Daming County in Hebei province.

12. Local poverty reduction teams, headed by an official with higher education and with a clear mandate and accountability, developed the specific local approaches. These teams would often spend several years in one location to develop local trust and understanding and adapt policy interventions to local needs. This approach was particularly important for the development of local economic opportunities, such as new production methods or the development of local processing and marketing capabilities for agricultural products.

13. These five areas are referred to as the "five-batch policies."

14. Working Plan on Poverty Registration, State Council Leading Group Office of Poverty Alleviation and Development, http://nrra.gov.cn/art/2014/4/11/art_624_14224.html.

15. Including the establishment in 2014 of the hotline "12317" for reporting poverty alleviation problems.

16. Data for provincial level funds for 2020 are not yet available.

17. These generally include industrial development for poverty alleviation, infrastructure improvement, vocational education and skills training programs for the poor, and subsidized loans and related management fees. Each province formulates a detailed list according to local conditions.

18. As of the end of 2021, all villages have access to broadband connections.

19. The coefficient on APF is also insignificant, though this may be due to the small sample size.

References

Alibaba Group. 2020. "Alibaba Poverty Relief Work Report 2020." July 2020. Alibaba, Hangzhou.

CIKD (Center for International Knowledge on Development). Forthcoming. *Economic Development and Poverty Alleviation in China*. Beijing: CIKD.

Freije-Rodriguez, Samuel, Bert Hofman, and Lauren Johnston. 2019. "Forty Years of China's Reforms, Poverty Reduction and the World Bank." East Asian Institute Working Paper, Singapore.

Freije-Rodriguez, Samuel, and Fuchang Zhao. 2021. "Public Expenditures under the 2011–2020 Poverty Reduction Strategy in China." In *Four Decades of Poverty Reduction in China: Background Papers*. Washington, DC: World Bank.

Hou, Xuejing. 2020. "Poverty Alleviation Office of the State Council: Exceeded the 200 Billion Yuan Annual Consumption Poverty Alleviation Task." Xinhaunet. September 11, 2020. http://www.xinhuanet.com/politics/2020-11/09/c_1126718314.htm.

ILO (International Labour Organization). 2015. "Universal Pension Coverage. People's Republic of China." Social Protection in Action. Building Social Protection Floors. ILO, Geneva.

Golan, John, T. Sicular, and N. Umapathi. 2017. "Unconditional Cash Transfers in China: Who Benefits from the Rural Minimum Living Standard Guarantee (Di Bao) Program?" *World Development* 93: 316–36.

Jiang, Xiheng, and Changyu Liu. 2020. "How Digital Technology Contributes to Poverty Reduction in China." *China Economic Times*, 20 August 2020.

Li, Shi, Peng Zhan, and Yangyang Shen. 2017. "New Patterns in China's Rural Poverty." Centre for Human Capital and Productivity Working Paper 2017-17, Department of Economics, University of Western Ontario, London, ON.

Liu, Mingyue, Xiaolong Feng, Sangui Wang, and Huanguang Qiu. 2020. "China's Poverty Alleviation over the Last 40 Years: Successes and Challenges." *Australian Journal of Agricultural and Resource Economics* 64 (1): 209–28.

Luo, Xubei, and Chiyu Niu. 2019. "E-Commerce Participation and Household Income Growth in Taobao Villages." Policy Research Working Paper 8811, World Bank, Washington, DC.

Meng, Lingsheng. 2013. "Evaluating China's Poverty Alleviation Program: A Regression Discontinuity Approach." *Journal of Public Economics* 101(C): 1–11.

Park, A., S. Wang, and G. Wu. 2002. "Regional Poverty Targeting in China." *Journal of Public Economics* 86 (1): 123–53.

State Council. 2021. *Poverty Alleviation: China's Experience and Contribution.* Beijing: The State Council Information Office of the People's Republic of China. http://english.www.gov.cn/archive/whitepaper/202104/06/content_WS606bc77ec6d0719374afc1b9.html.

Tang, Lixia, and Yang Liu. 2020. "Analysis on Development and Evolution of Chinese Targeted Poverty Alleviation." *Journal of Hubei University (Philosophy and Social Science)* 47 (5): 133–41.

Wang, Meiyan, Xiaobo Qu, and Peng Jia. 2017. "Roles of Rural Di Bao/Social Assistance and Area-Based Antipoverty Programs in Eradicating China's Rural Poverty." Institute of Population and Labor Economics, Chinese Academy of Social Sciences (CASS), Beijing.

Wang, Sangui, Zhou Li, and Yanshun Ren. 2004. "The 8-7 National Poverty Reduction Program in China: The National Strategy and Its Impact." World Bank Group, Washington, DC.

Wang, Sangui, Albert Park, Shubham Chaudhuri, and Gaurav Datt. 2007. "Poverty Alleviation and Community-Based Development in China." *Journal of Management World* 1: 56–64.

Westmore, B. 2017. "Do Government Transfers Reduce Poverty in China? Micro Evidence from Five Regions." OECD Economics Department Working Paper 1415, OECD, Paris.

World Bank. 1992. *China: Strategies for Reducing Poverty in the 1990s.* Washington, DC: World Bank.

World Bank. 2001. *China: Overcoming Rural Poverty.* A World Bank country study. Washington, DC: World Bank.

World Bank. 2009. *China—From Poor Areas to Poor People: China's Evolving Poverty Reduction Agenda—An Assessment of Poverty and Inequality.* Washington, DC: World Bank.

World Bank. 2020. *Infrastructure in Asia and the Pacific: Road Transport, Electricity, and Water and Sanitation Services in East Asia, South Asia, and the Pacific Islands.* Washington, DC: World Bank.

World Bank. 2021. *"Social Assistance Programs in China: Current State and Directions for Reform."* Technical note, World Bank, Washington, DC.

World Bank. Forthcoming. *Four Decades of Poverty Reduction in China: Background Papers.* Washington, DC: World Bank.

World Bank and Alibaba Group. 2019. *E-commerce Development: Experience from China: Overview.* Washington, DC: World Bank Group.

Xi, Jinping. 2021. "Speech at a National Conference to Review the Fight against Poverty and Commend Individuals and Groups Involved." Central Compilation & Translation Press, Beijing.

Zhou, Yang, Yuanzhi Guo, and Yansui Liu. 2020. "Health, Income and Poverty: Evidence from China's Rural Household Survey." *International Journal for Equity in Health* 19: 36.

5

Implications of China's Poverty Reduction

China's approach to poverty reduction in a global context

Although China's rapid economic growth benefited from some favorable initial conditions (including a relatively well-educated and healthy population, low fertility rates, high savings rates, and equitable land distribution), the story of poverty reduction following economic transformation is not unique to China. Indeed, the policy lessons emerging from this experience are consistent with those from other high-growth episodes in East Asia (such as Japan, the Republic of Korea, and Singapore). These lessons include a focus on education, outward orientation, public investments in infrastructure, macroeconomic stability, and structural policies broadly consistent with comparative advantage and supportive of competition (see World Bank [2009] on economic growth, and Ravallion [2009, 2011] on its importance for poverty reduction). The beginning of reforms in agriculture, using the gains in productivity and incomes as a catalyst to drive a subsequent labor-intensive industrialization and urbanization process, offers an important lesson in the sequencing of development processes, of broader application to low-income countries.

China's experience echoes that of other East Asian countries in two other respects. The first is China's preference for development-oriented poverty reduction over redistribution. This preference is grounded in the belief that employment creation should be the main driver of poverty reduction. Specific policies directing sizable transfers to poor areas and—later—to poor people emerged 10 years after the start of the reforms and took prominence in the past decade, as the country's poverty rate fell below 10 percent. Nevertheless, and despite the recent expansion, social transfers have low benefit rates and the bulk of assistance is provided in kind. Social insurance coverage is wider than in the past, but benefit levels for noncontributory programs are still relatively low. Instead, China, like other countries in East Asia, has spent large public resources on infrastructure investments to improve connectivity and support investment and job creation. This strategy has served China well up to its present level of income. But like the "East Asian tigers" before it, China will need to find new drivers of growth going forward, and as the economy shifts toward innovation and services, the role of social protection systems to encourage risk-taking and cushion those left behind by rapid structural change is likely to increase.

Second, China, like Japan, Korea, and Singapore, has been endowed with a "capable and effective government" (Bikales 2021; Ravallion 2009), as reflected in the ability to articulate credible policy commitments, to effectively coordinate decisions by various government departments, and to mobilize a variety of social actors to support a national goal. China's various poverty reduction campaigns illustrate these mechanisms well and show how the underlying functions of China's governance institutions are quite similar to those of other successful development cases, even if the policies and the historical context are different (box 5.1; for a comprehensive treatment of these issues, see World Bank [2017]).

On the other hand, the policy context in which the economic transformation took place clearly differed between China and its peers. In part, this reflects China's size and diversity, which led to a greater emphasis on gradualism with experimentation and policy discovery as a result of interprovincial competition (rather than central policy design). In part, it reflects caution against relinquishing government control too much or too quickly (Naughton 2018).

China's ability to experiment and learn from pilots has clearly been an important advantage for creating conditions for adaptation. The gradualism adopted by China in reforming the economy (associated with Deng Xiaoping saying "Crossing the river by feeling the stones") was reflected in the incremental approach toward the liberalization of agricultural and industrial product markets, the managed approach toward migration and urbanization, and a much larger role for the state in ownership of key assets and the allocation of resources than in other market economies. China's vastly different initial conditions complicate the comparison with other cases of economic transition, such as in the former Soviet Union or Eastern Europe (Raiser 1995). Nonetheless, gradual reforms, consistent with a growing role for competition and markets, may have facilitated the adaptation of business and people to the scale and speed of China's economic transformation. The persistent efforts needed to convince farmers to adopt new production technologies, as described in box 3.1, may serve as an example.

Cautious reforms were complemented with experimentation, allowing the country to adjust policy when faced with evidence that it was not working (Ang 2016; Kanbur and Zhang 2009). Local policy autonomy (inherited from the prereform era) served as an incentive for local institutional innovations in an arrangement known as "experimentation under hierarchy" (Heilmann 2008) or "directed improvisation" (Ang 2016). The introduction of the household responsibility system, reforms of the township and village enterprises, and the creation of special economic zones all started as part of successful local pilots later scaled up nationwide.

One of the emerging lessons from China's experience is the importance of building targeted support on the foundation of robust evidence. In the 1990s, this involved the use of household budget surveys to identify poor counties and later villages and target development efforts accordingly. In the most recent targeted poverty reduction campaign, China started with a comprehensive survey of its poor households, which allowed resources to be directed to where they would have the biggest impact, differentiating among households in terms of the most binding constraints to improving their economic opportunities. The census represented a central element of the coordination and implementation of government policies at the local level and in principle allowed regular monitoring and evaluation. This element of China's approach could be further strengthened by allowing more outside researchers to access and analyze the vast data collected in China's poverty registry.

Some specific policies chosen by China to tackle the social dimensions of the economic transformation continue to be hotly debated among development economists; therefore, the implications for other countries remain unclear. These include, among others, issues such as China's urbanization policies (specifically the role of the *hukou*). An evaluation of these policy choices was not part of the scope of this study. Suffice to add a few retrospective reflections.

Managed urbanization was an objective of China's policy makers early on. The intention was to limit the growth of large cities to avoid the emergence of urban poverty through the uncontrolled development of slums, while at the same time providing sufficient

BOX 5.1   China's poverty reduction policies as a case study in pro-poor governance[a]

It has long been recognized that a capable, credible, and committed government is key to the success of development strategies. The 2017 World Development Report (World Bank 2017) aims to break down the core functions of effective governance to draw lessons for development. Its main message is that effective governance institutions deliver three core functions: *credible commitment, enhancing coordination, **and inducing cooperation.*** All three core functions were present in the design and implementation of China's poverty reduction efforts, which represents an interesting case study of effective governance.

First, *the credibility of the government's commitment* to poverty reduction was signaled early on, with clearly defined targets and the creation of the Leading Group on Poverty Alleviation and Development to oversee progress and establish accountability at the highest level. When it became clear that economic growth alone would not suffice to reach the last mile of poverty reduction, President Xi declared the eradication of absolute poverty to be one of his "three decisive battles" and set it as a key target of the 13th Five-Year Plan (2016–2020). With this rallying call it became clear that failure was not an option (Freije-Rodriguez, Hofman, and Johnston 2019).

Second, the use of incentives played a very important role in *facilitating coordination* across different levels of government. Since 2013, the membership of the Leading Group on Poverty Alleviation and Development has been expanded to include all central ministries and departments, reflecting the importance placed on interdepartmental coordination. While the central government through the Leading Group provided broad guidance, local officials were given wide latitude to experiment and indeed compete with each other (Ang 2016; Heilmann 2008). Clearly defined reward and accountability mechanisms, with a strong performance management system, ensured that cadres aligned personal goals with central priorities (Xu 2011). Career promotion of local officials depended on their performance in achieving predefined outcomes (for example, economic growth, social stability, or poverty reduction). With the launch of the poverty reduction campaign, poverty reduction targets in the designated poor counties became one of the top performance

evaluation criteria for local officials, with poverty reduction management teams delegated from higher levels of government to poor villages and counties with the exclusive task of working toward the goal and monitoring and reporting on progress made. While there have been reports of local collusion, fraud, and diversion of resources, tight supervision and unannounced inspections from higher levels have on the whole ensured strong compliance. Fiscal incentives reinforced the performance management targets, encouraging local governments to mobilize the resources necessary to achieve their goals. Poverty reduction is one of the few areas in which China has experimented with programmatic budgeting, allowing the governments of 832 poverty-stricken counties to pool resources across several departments, prioritized in line with local requirements (World Bank 2018).

Third, China has adopted a whole-of-government and whole-of-society approach, particularly in the latest phase of the poverty eradication campaign, which is *inducing cooperation across government and nongovernment stakeholders.* The poverty reduction campaign (like the COVID-19 [coronavirus] containment efforts more recently) is a good example of China's approach to social mobilization, including cadres at all levels, state and privately owned enterprises, academic institutions, and others. These stakeholders were encouraged to make substantial financial and human resource contributions to the poverty reduction campaign. Participation is perceived as a patriotic duty (Freije-Rodriguez and Zhao 2021). One example of this social mobilization and induced cooperation across stakeholders is the "East-West Cooperation for Poverty Reduction" described in box 4.3.

Although the governance functions exemplified by China's poverty reduction efforts can be applied to many development contexts, the specific institutions developed in China are arguably unique. For example, few countries would have the mobilization capacity of party cadres at all levels of government. Moreover, China's governance mechanisms, while effective at reaching specific targets, such as economic growth or poverty reduction, confront challenges when dealing with multiple objectives requiring trade-offs across priorities (World Bank and DRC 2019).

a. This box builds primarily on CIKD (forthcoming, chapter 9), and World Bank (2017).

opportunities for the rural poor to improve their incomes (and those of their families remaining in the village) through migration. Critics of these policies point to the human costs it generated, the potential negative impact on social mobility and equality of opportunity it had, and the underutilized potential of agglomeration economies in China's large cities (World Bank and DRC 2014). In the absence of a credible counterfactual, the question of whether the benefits of China's restrictions of population movements have exceeded their costs needs to remain open. As the pressures to migrate have receded, the restrictions have been progressively lifted. Even if the hukou has played a positive role in coordinating the pace of urban migration and job creation and reducing the pressure on urban services in the past, in the face of the economic inequalities that it risks perpetuating, the time may have come to lift it altogether.

China has relied heavily on public investment in infrastructure to support long-term development and to boost the economy during downturns. The evidence presented in this report points to significant positive spillover effects for all sectors of the economy and for poverty reduction. However, with significant service gaps remaining in rural areas, particularly with respect to health care and education services, the bias in local government incentives toward investments in hard infrastructure to boost growth and the reliance on land-based financing vehicles arguably perpetuates a misallocation of fiscal resources that could be costly in the long term (World Bank and DRC 2019). The environmental footprint of China's infrastructure explosion adds to concerns that the country will need a different, more services-oriented growth model going forward. The challenges of managing the transition to a greener and more inclusive development path and the implications for poverty reduction and social policies are examined in the next chapter of this synthesis report.

References

Ang, Yuen Yuen. 2016. *How China Escaped the Poverty Trap.* Ithaca, NY: Cornell University Press.

Bikales, B. 2021. "Reflections on Poverty Reduction in China." Swiss Agency for Development and Cooperation, Bern.

CIKD (Center for International Knowledge on Development). Forthcoming. *Economic Development and Poverty Alleviation in China.* Beijing: CIKD.

Freije-Rodriguez, Samuel, Bert Hofman, and Lauren Johnston. 2019. "China's Economic Reforms, Poverty Reduction, and the Role of the World Bank." East Asia Institute Working Paper, Seoul.

Freije-Rodriguez, Samuel, and Fuchang Zhao. 2021. "Public Expenditures under the 2011–2020 Poverty Reduction Strategy in China." In *Four Decades of Poverty Reduction in China: Background Papers.* Washington, DC: World Bank.

Heilmann, Sebastian. 2008. "Policy Experimentation in China's Economic Rise." *Studies in Comparative International Development* 43: 1–26.

Kanbur, Ravi, and Xiaobo Zhang, eds. 2009. *Governing Rapid Growth in China: Equity and Institutions.* Oxfordshire, UK: Routledge.

Naughton, Barry. 2018. *The Chinese Economy: Adaptation and Growth.* Second edition. Cambridge, MA: MIT Press.

Raiser, Martin. 1995. "'Transition Is a Bridge, Therefore Do Not Dwell upon It.'" *Economics of Transition* 3 (2): 215–46.

Ravallion, Martin. 2009. "Are There Lessons for Africa from China's Success against Poverty?" *World Development* 37 (2): 303–31.

Ravallion, Martin. 2011. "A Comparative Perspective on Poverty Reduction in Brazil, China, and India." *World Bank Research Observer* 26 (1): 71–104.

World Bank. 2009. *China—From Poor Areas to Poor People: China's Evolving Poverty Reduction Agenda—An Assessment of Poverty and Inequality.* Washington, DC: World Bank.

World Bank. 2017. *World Development Report 2017: Governance and the Law.* Washington, DC: World Bank.

World Bank. 2018. *"Guangxi Poverty Reduction Program-for-Results Project."* World Bank Group, Washington, DC.

World Bank and DRC (Development Research Center of the State Council). 2014. *Urban China: Toward Efficient, Inclusive, and Sustainable Urbanization.* Washington, DC: World Bank.

World Bank and DRC (Development Research Center of the State Council). 2019. *Innovative China: New Drivers of Growth.* Washington, DC: World Bank.

Xu, Chenggang. 2011. "The Fundamental Institutions of China's Reforms and Development." *Journal of Economic Literature* 49 (4): 1076–151.

6

The Way Ahead

Introduction

China has come a long way from being a low-income, predominantly agrarian economy to the upper-middle-income industrial powerhouse that it is today. Over the past four decades, the definitions of what it means to be poor in China have been continuously adapted to the changing economic reality, and policies to address poverty have correspondingly shifted. Looking ahead, China's economy faces major new structural changes that will require the country's approach to poverty reduction to change yet again.

This chapter explores three themes that are likely to shape the debate over poverty reduction going forward: (1) the future patterns of growth and structural change, including the shift to a service economy, the growing role of domestic consumption, the need for adjustments to reach China's net zero carbon commitments, and the projected rapid aging of China's population; (2) the evolution of China's poverty standard as incomes rise further; and (3) the integration of China's poverty reduction policies with its social protection system more generally, to account for poverty risks stemming from the increasingly transient nature of employment in a modern economy and the need to support and facilitate the rapid structural changes that lie ahead.

China's past lessons provide some orientation for the future. But China will do well to continue to study the experiences of today's advanced economies when they were upper-middle income. One lesson from that experience is clear: whether the resulting prosperity is shared and benefits the worse off as much as the better off remains a key yardstick for development success.

New drivers of growth and poverty reduction

The process of economic transformation and urbanization in China has not completely run its course. The share of agriculture in employment remains high, while the rate of urbanization is relatively low, especially expressed as a share of the population in large megacities. Some potential thus remains for further productivity gains via reallocation of labor across sectors and locations.

Nonetheless, China will not be able to rely on the same drivers of growth to boost incomes further and achieve lasting improvements for the less well-off among its citizens (World Bank and DRC 2019). Increased levels of debt, concerns about the environmental footprint of the past growth model, and the diminishing pool of available labor resources due to rapid population aging dampen growth prospects going forward. Growth can no longer rely on capital deepening and low wages to the same extent as in the past—future increases in productivity will need to come from innovations and the greater diffusion of new technologies. In other words, the Chinese economy needs to rebalance from an investment- and export-led model based on labor-intensive manufacturing toward one led by domestic consumption, services, and increases in productivity. In China, currently the share of services in consumer demand is about 40–41 percent for those in the bottom 40 percent of household incomes, but rises to 51 percent in the top decile. In contrast, in upper-middle-income and high-income countries, health, education, entertainment, transport and communication, housing, and other services make up, on average, between 70 percent and 80 percent of private household consumption. There is thus considerable scope for moving to high-value-added services as the new engine of income growth and job creation. The policies needed to support such a shift are also different, requiring greater liberalization and competition in the service sector, the harnessing of the full potential of China's large cities as hubs for service-based innovation, and improvements in skills, including to adjust to the coming digital age.

The required structural shift in China's growth model will receive additional impetus from the imperative to scale up climate action. China has made a clear commitment to achieve the emissions peak by 2030 and reach carbon neutrality by 2060. This represents a major policy shift with near-term ramifications. Achieving a greener, more sustainable China in turn implies a deep economic and social transformation that will not only affect the use and management of China's natural assets but induce a reallocation of all factors of production, transforming the structure of demand (consumption) and supply (production). Incidentally, a move toward a more service-based economy would support a reduced carbon footprint, but cities, as the hubs of service-based innovation, will need to plan for a zero-carbon future. Although decarbonization entails transition risks and costs, it also presents an opportunity to spur innovation, job creation, and growth. Reforms can be poverty reducing and equity enhancing if the necessary mechanisms are put in place. Policies to ease labor mobility, strengthen the social safety net, and provide alternative sources of income to those affected by the transition can play a central role. A carbon emissions trading system could reduce the emissions in a market-based approach with a declining cap.

China's aging workforce points to the importance of deepening the accumulation of human capital. The dramatic reduction in the dependency rate due to falling fertility contributed significantly to poverty reduction over the past decades. However, the demographic window has been closing since 2010. The size of the labor force has already started to shrink nationwide, and aging is happening earlier and faster in rural areas. Based on current trends, by 2050 the demographic dependency rate in China will reach 67.3 percent of the population, which is above the projected US level of 63.7 percent for the same year. The new generations will have to economically and socially sustain the growing aged population. The increase in old-age dependency will start to put the brakes on rural poverty reduction unless social policies are adjusted to mitigate this effect.

With average working hours declining (a trend observed in all countries as they develop), and with the end of the demographic dividend, to maintain its labor input China will need to look to increase labor force participation and increase the quality of the workforce. There is scope for both, especially as labor conditions and wages improve. Despite the priority Chinese policy makers attach to human capital formation, significant challenges remain. The gap in the quality of education between poor rural and richer urban areas is wide. Despite equalization transfers, differences in local revenue mobilization are driving education budgets at the school level. Closing the gap will require investments in education, especially in rural areas. In addition, as most of the workforce is already out of school, reforms to promote adult education and retraining programs such as night-school diplomas and life-long learning to allow workers to upgrade their skills are also required.

Defining new standards and policy objectives for a prosperous China

It has been known since Adam Smith that what constitutes poverty is ultimately a function of the society a person lives in.[1] The World Bank's absolute poverty line of US$1.90 per day in purchasing power parity (PPP) terms is derived from the national poverty lines of the poorest countries in the world, representing the cost of a minimum daily calorific intake and the computed needs for basic shelter and clothing in these societies. The idea is that this line can be viewed as an absolute minimum threshold for defining poverty in all countries (World Bank 2018). As countries grow richer, however, this standard is no longer adequate for measuring poverty or determining appropriate levels of assistance. Accordingly, national poverty lines tend to increase with growing per capita income (Joliffe and Prydz 2016). China has adjusted its own poverty line three times over the past 40 years to the present level of US$2.30 per day. Globally, to take these shifts into account, the World Bank has since 2016 recommended the use of three different internationally comparable poverty lines that are typically found in low-income, lower-middle-income, and upper-middle-income countries. For the latter, the recommended internationally comparable poverty line is US$5.50 per person per day (in 2011 PPP).

In other words, China's journey in poverty reduction did not end with the eradication of absolute poverty in 2020. With the adoption of a concept of poverty better suited to a moderately prosperous society, some 200 million people would still require support to realize improved living standards. A key policy decision will be how to set the new poverty standard. There is no unique way of doing this. Some countries use a higher absolute poverty line based on the cost of basic needs (the United States' poverty line, for instance, is set at US$21.70 a day in 2011 PPP); others prefer relative poverty lines (most of the European countries set their minimum living standard as 50 percent or 60 percent of median disposable income), and some countries use multidimensional poverty measures (as in Mexico, combining monetary and nonmonetary dimensions).

The shift toward a higher poverty standard will have implications for the nature of government policies. First, with a higher threshold, the growth of employment opportunities and labor incomes is likely once again to become a key driver of poverty reduction. Indeed, between 2007 and 2018 almost one-third of poverty reduction, if measured at the higher line of US$5.50 per day, was due to increases in labor income. By contrast, for the extreme poor, labor income made an insignificant contribution to poverty reduction. Second, the inclusiveness of economic growth will matter significantly for the future path of poverty reduction. The first three decades of reform and opening up in China were accompanied by rapid increases in inequality. In the past decade, the trend toward rising inequality has begun to turn around (Kanbur, Wang, and Zhang 2021) as rural-urban wage gaps have declined, and poorer regions have grown faster, on average, than richer ones. However, this reversal has been earned at the cost of huge capital investment, not all of it productive (World Bank 2020), and inequality levels remain high for an aspiring high-income economy. Additional policy efforts may thus be needed to sustain the decline in inequality.

It should be noted that policies that address the root cause of the prevailing inequality can support not only poverty reduction but also economic growth. At the time Japan, the Republic of Korea, and the United States became high-income economies, the share of national income going to the top 10 percent was significantly lower than what it is now in

China (Dixon and Gill 2021). A larger share of income for the bottom of the distribution could spur a more consumption-based growth model, as poorer households tend to spend a larger share of their marginal income. In addition, a more equal distribution of economic opportunities would ensure that China loses less of its human capital potential at a time when its labor force has started to decline. Closing gaps in access to quality public services will be key to ensuring equal economic opportunities and increased social mobility for future generations. In addition, progressive tax systems can play an important role in addressing inequality and relative poverty, as they do in Organisation for Economic Co-operation and Development (OECD) countries. A study shows that the personal income tax in China is, indeed, equalizing, but its effect on inequality is minor (Lustig and Wang 2020). Progressive personal income tax accounts for only 5 percent of revenue in China, while yielding close to 15 percent, on average, in the OECD.

Coordinating pro-poor development policies and social protection programs

The Chinese authorities are well aware of the challenges lying ahead to sustain the gains in poverty reduction. At the beginning of 2021, the government announced a strategic shift from poverty alleviation to rural revitalization, transforming the key institution, the Leading Group on Poverty Alleviation and Development, into the National Rural Revitalization Administration. In adopting this approach, the government has confirmed the priority it continues to place on the social and economic vulnerabilities experienced by China's rural population. Concerned with the persistently high rural-urban income gap, the rural revitalization strategy focuses both on modernizing China's agriculture to boost agricultural productivity growth and make it environmentally more sustainable, and on modernizing the rural economy in general, including through improved public services and the creation and retention of nonagricultural rural jobs. To buttress the commitment to the rural areas and households that only recently rose above the absolute poverty threshold, the authorities have committed to maintain funding levels provided during the poverty eradication campaign for a transition period of five years. This commitment will ensure that the rural revitalization strategy is adequately resourced with central and provincial government transfers in the face of still very limited own fiscal resources in rural villages and counties.

While the continued focus on rural areas is clearly justified, living standards in urban areas also need to be closely monitored. Nationwide, about one-third of the poor in 2018, identified using the US$5.50 poverty line, lived in urban areas, and this share is increasing. Therefore, the emphasis on rural revitalization should be complemented with efforts to support job creation and strengthen social protection mechanisms for the urban poor, including many informal and migrant workers for which consumption poverty is significant (Guo, Tan, and Qu 2018). The required policy mechanisms will differ between the rural and the urban poor, given that the latter tend to be more integrated into the modern economy and face different types of shocks, such as temporary unemployment, loss of shelter, and additional spending needs, such as on public transport and shelter, as well as on education and health services for those without urban *hukous*. At the same time, their poverty spells may be more transient than structural, requiring more limited periods of assistance to bridge temporary difficulties and prevent a downward spiral.

The changing profile of China's poor during the next stage of development highlights the need to better integrate targeted poverty reduction and institutionalized social protection policies. As shown in chapter 4, although the coverage of social safety nets in China has broadened significantly, informal and migrant workers fall outside most government support policies and thus remain highly vulnerable.[2] Social assistance programs such as the Di Bao could help here. They mobilize a similar fiscal effort (about 0.2 percent of gross domestic product [GDP] per year) as targeted poverty alleviation (which cumulatively over 2013–20 amounted to 1.5 GDP [see State Council 2021]) and focus on the same beneficiaries in terms of income. However, the National Poverty Registry managed by the Leading Group Office of Poverty Alleviation and Development and the Social Assistance Registry managed by the Ministry of Civil Affairs remain separate. During the targeted poverty reduction strategy, efforts were made at the local government level to triangulate information obtained from both databases (as discussed for Guizhou in box 4.4, for example), but these remained partial. The emphasis on the "dynamic monitoring" of population living conditions going forward will require deeper integration. Such integration could bring efficiency gains that would help increase the adequacy of social protection benefits more generally, particularly for rural pensions, which, despite rapid growth in coverage, remain at a fraction of the rural poverty line.

A more integrated social protection system would also better protect households in both urban and rural areas from shocks. The government's response to the COVID-19 (coronavirus) pandemic has offered an opportunity to explore the new avenues for social policy. China has made unprecedented efforts to provide protection from vulnerability to migrants living and working in urban areas, covering them with income support to compensate for lost wages. Removal of financial barriers to health care access during the COVID-19 mitigation effort benefited both individuals and communities. These policy innovations made in times of crisis provide useful experiences for the possible way forward for China's post-2020 poverty alleviation agenda.

Notes

1. In Adam Smith's time, a person was considered poor if she could not even afford a linen shirt.
2. The processes of assessing exclusion error in the existing registries themselves may benefit from an evaluation. Although much effort at the local level is deployed to keep them dynamic and up to date, more evidence can help to further improve them.

References

Dixon, Eric L., and Indermit S. Gill. 2021. "Poverty in China as Its Economy Nears High Income: Lessons from Japan, South Korea and the United States during Their Upper-Middle Income Transitions." Duke Global Working Paper Series 34, Duke University, Durham, NC.

Guo, Junping, Qingxiang Tan, and Song Qu. 2018. "The Poverty of Rural Migrant Families: An Analytical Framework from the Perspectives of Income, Consumption and Multi-dimensions." *China Rural Economy* (9): 1–16.

Jolliffe, Dean, and Espen Prydz. 2016. "Estimating International Poverty Lines from Comparable National Thresholds." *Journal of Economic Inequality* 14: 185–98.

Kanbur, Ravi, Yue Wang, and Xiaobo Zhang. 2021. "The Great Chinese Inequality Turnaround." *Journal of Comparative Economics* 49 (2): 467–82.

Lustig, Nora, and Yang Wang. 2020. "The Impact of Taxes and Transfers on Income Inequality, Poverty, and the Urban-Rural and Regional Income Gaps in China." Commitment to Equity Working Paper Series 93, Tulane University, Department of Economics, New Orleans, LA.

State Council. 2021. *Poverty Alleviation: China's Experience and Contribution.* Beijing: The State Council Information Office of the People's Republic of China. http://english.www.gov.cn/archive/whitepaper/202104/06/content_WS606bc77ec6d0719374afc1b9.html.

World Bank. 2018. *Poverty and Shared Prosperity 2018: Piecing Together the Poverty Puzzle.* Washington, DC: World Bank.

World Bank. 2020. *Infrastructure in Asia and the Pacific: Road Transport, Electricity, and Water and Sanitation Services in East Asia, South Asia, and the Pacific Islands.* Washington, DC: World Bank.

World Bank and DRC (Development Research Center of the State Council). 2019. *Innovative China: New Drivers of Growth.* Washington, DC: World Bank.

7

Conclusions

Concluding remarks

What has China achieved? Over the past 40 years, the number of people in China with incomes below US$1.90 per day—the World Bank's absolute poverty line—has fallen by close to 800 million. With this, China has accounted for more than 70 percent of the global reduction in the number of people living in extreme poverty. China's poverty reduction is historically unprecedented in speed and scale. Although China has eradicated extreme poverty, a significant number of people remain vulnerable, with incomes below a threshold more typically used to define poverty in upper-middle-income countries. Thus, it may take some years to consolidate the progress of poverty reduction.

What were the drivers of China's poverty reduction? China's poverty reduction story is primarily a growth story. Rapid economic growth since the launch of reform and opening up in 1978 can partially be attributed to favorable initial conditions, including a relatively well-educated and healthy population, low fertility rates, and equitable land distribution. China shared some of these characteristics with other fast-growing economies, particularly those in East Asia, and to some extent the pace of poverty reduction since 1980 reflects China catching up with regional peers.

China's rapid and sustained economic growth has been accompanied by a broad-based economic transformation. Reforms began in the agricultural sector, where the poor could benefit directly from improvements in productivity associated with the introduction of market incentives. The development of low-skilled, labor-intensive industries provided a source of employment for workers released from agriculture. Urbanization helped migrants take advantage of the new opportunities in the cities, and migrant worker transfers boosted household incomes in townships and villages as well. Public investment in infrastructure improved living conditions in rural areas but also connected them with urban and export markets. Reforms in all these areas were incremental, which may have helped businesses and the population adjust to the rapid pace of change. When the poverty headcount dropped below 10 percent of the rural population, targeted poverty alleviation and social protection systems started playing a more important role. After 2013, concerted policy efforts to reach the last mile, involving substantial government transfers as well as the mobilization of resources from a variety of stakeholders, contributed to the eradication of extreme poverty.

What could China offer for the global poverty reduction effort? China's success in poverty reduction holds lessons at both the macro and micro levels. First, China's macroeconomic growth trajectory mirrors key findings of comparative work on sustained high growth. The ingredients of success in those developing countries that have grown 7 percent or more per year for over 25 years include an emphasis on human capital accumulation, outward orientation, public investments in infrastructure, macroeconomic stability, and structural policies generally consistent with comparative advantages and supportive of competition (Commission on Growth and Development 2008). China's sequencing of reforms, beginning in agriculture, where the biggest immediate productivity and income gains could be achieved, also mattered. Of course, good ingredients do not on their own make a tasty dish. The second macro-level lesson, therefore, is that China fashioned policies consistent with the above principles to fit its specific institutional context. For China, a high-level commitment to growth, development, and poverty reduction has played a key role in policy coordination. China's use of performance incentives and targets to drive policy implementation while at the same time allowing for significant local experimentation and entrepreneurship to achieve macro policy objectives provides an important case study in effective governance.

At the micro level, China's experience offers a number of lessons: how to use agricultural extension as a driver of technological progress in on- and off-farm production, how to leverage the power of e-commerce together with a strong domestic logistics network to integrate rural areas into urban supply chains, how to finance connectivity and urban development based on the rising value of land that comes with economic transformation, and how to use repeated survey evidence to identify poor regions and households and target government interventions according to needs. Some of these micro lessons are summarized in the boxes throughout this synthesis report; others are contained in the case study background papers; yet others have been captured in the existing literature (Liu at al. 2020; Ravallion 2009). However, much remains to be done to better understand not just the what but the how to of China's successes and thereby help other countries benefit from China's lessons.

What lessons does China's past offer for the future? The eradication of extreme poverty is not the end of China's poverty reduction agenda in a broader sense. China's government has renewed its commitment to sustaining past gains through the adoption of its rural revitalization strategy, with the objective of bringing common prosperity to both urban and rural areas and further integrating their respective economies. Against this background, it is likely that China's policy toward poverty reduction will remain *development oriented* and emphasize the creation of jobs and economic opportunities over the provision of social welfare. The adoption of a higher poverty threshold more in line with China's current average level of per capita income could be part of this approach, because it would once again make rising wage earnings a key driver of poverty reduction. To ensure equal opportunities for all in the face of a rapidly changing labor market, the remaining gaps in access to quality services (in particular, education services) would need to be closed. The integration of targeted poverty reduction efforts with China's existing social assistance instruments could bring further efficiency and help mitigate the risks for the most vulnerable associated with the expected continued economic transformation toward a greener, more urban, and more service-oriented economy.

In what direction should further research into China's poverty reduction head? An evaluation of China's targeted poverty alleviation experience in recent years would benefit from further analysis of individual policy interventions and their interactions to better understand not just the effectiveness but also the efficiency and sustainability of the program. An analysis of the costs and benefits of policy intervention would also be warranted in a broader sense, helping to systematically account (*suan da zhang* in Chinese) for factors such as the impact of infrastructure investments on poverty reduction or the merits of the *hukou* system and China's managed urbanization policies. In all these areas, active exchanges between researchers within and outside of China and between academics and policy makers should be encouraged, and the data needed for high-quality empirical work should be made more widely available. This will help ensure that China's poverty reduction achievements get the attention that they deserve.

References

Commission on Growth and Development. 2008. *The Growth Report: Strategies for Sustained Growth and Inclusive Development.* Washington, DC: World Bank.

Liu, Mingyue, Xiaolong Feng, Sangui Wang, and Huanguang Qiu. 2020. "China's Poverty Alleviation over the Last 40 Years: Successes and Challenges." *Australian Journal of Agricultural and Resource Economics* 64 (1): 209–28.

Ravallion, Martin. 2009. "Are There Lessons for Africa from China's Success against Poverty?" *World Development* 37 (2): 303–31.

Appendix A:
Key Household Surveys

Throughout the report, several sources of information on household and individual's well-being are used, some of them used extensively by the authors of the background papers. This appendix describes their main characteristics.

National Survey of Household Income and Expenditure and Living Conditions. Collected by the National Bureau of Statistics (NBS), this survey is used for obtaining information on income, expenditure and living conditions of urban and rural residents. From a sampling frame from the population census, 160,000 households are selected across urban and rural areas, based on place of residence. Until 2012, the NBS implemented separate urban and rural household surveys. In 2013, they were integrated into a single survey. The sampling frame changed, from relying on registration (*hukou*) to being based on population census. With this change, rural migrant workers that have been working and residing in a city over six consecutive months were reclassified as being members of the urban population. Households record information on income and expenditure using a diary for a full year. The survey is used to measure key indicators such as average disposable income, per capita expenditure, poverty incidence in rural areas, and the Gini coefficient, among others. The main results are presented in the China Statistical Yearbook and the China Household Survey Yearbook, published yearly by the NBS. For more information, see http://www.stats.gov.cn/tjzs/cjwtjd/201308/t20130829_74325.html.

National Rural Poverty Monitoring Survey. The NBS also carries out a similar household survey in rural poverty-stricken areas identified in the "Outline of China's Rural Poverty Alleviation and Development (2011–2020)." The purpose is to reflect the poverty situation in contiguous poverty-stricken areas and key counties in poverty alleviation and development work, and compare the income growth, infrastructure, and basic public services of rural residents in poverty-stricken areas and the country. The results are reported in the annual China Rural Poverty Monitoring Reports, produced by the NBS.

RCRE Household Panel Survey (National Fixed-Point Survey), carried out by the Research Center for Rural Economy, Ministry of Agriculture in China. This is a nationally representative household survey that has been collected continuously since 1986. The survey collects detailed household-level information on incomes and expenditures through a daily diary, in addition to information on education, labor supply, asset ownership, landholdings, savings, formal and informal access to credit, and remittances. Because of its structure, the survey provides a long panel of villages across rural China.

Rural-Urban Migration in China is a longitudinal survey, conducted annually since 2008. It was initiated by a group of researchers at the Australian National University, the University of Queensland, and Beijing Normal University. The survey collects data about migrants' health, education, employment, social networks, household income and expenditure, housing conditions, and place of origin. The annual sample size consists of 5,000 migrant households living in 15 cities across 9 major provinces with the highest level of rural-to-urban migration. For more information, see https://sdc-iesr.jnu.edu.cn/wome_16220/main.htm.

Chinese Household Income Project (CHIP). This project is part of the activities carried out by the China Institute for Income Distribution of Beijing Normal University. The CHIP survey is implemented by a mix of research institutions and academics in coordination with the NBS. There are six rounds (1988, 1995, 2002, 2007, 2013, 2018) covering rural and urban areas. The survey is representative at the urban/rural level and regional level (four regions). CHIP surveys are a good alternative to official data when micro data are not available, particularly if the aim is to cover a long period. They are a subsample of the official rural, urban, and integrated household surveys described above. Households are revisited to implement the CHIP questionnaire, which captures rich information on hukou registration, education, social insurance, employment and job characteristics, retirement conditions, education and occupation of parents of heads of households, as well as subjective well-being. For more information, see http://www.ciidbnu.org/chip/index.asp?lang=EN; Gustafsson, Shi, and Sicular (2008); and Li, Sato, and Sicular (2013).

References

Gustafsson, Björn A., Li Shi, and Terry Sicular, eds. 2008. *Inequality and Public Policy in China.* Cambridge and New York: Cambridge University Press.

Li, Shi, Hiroshi Sato, and Terry Sicular, eds. 2013. *Rising Inequality in China: Challenges to a Harmonious Society.* Cambridge: Cambridge University Press.